NATIONAL
GEOGRAPHIC
KiDS

Funny
FiLL-IN

MY INSIDE THE EARTH ADVENTURE

NATIONAL GEOGRAPHIC
WASHINGTON, D.C.

How to Play Funny Fill-In!

Love to create amazing stories? Good, because this one stars YOU. Get ready to laugh with all your friends—you can play with as many people as you want! Make sure to keep this book on your shelf. You'll want to read it again and again!

Are You Ready to Laugh?

- One person picks a story—you can start at the beginning, the middle, or the end of the book.

- Ask a friend to call out a word that the space asks for—noun, verb, or something else—and write it in the blank space. If there's more than one player, ask the next person to say a word. Extra points for creativity!

- When all the spaces are filled in, you have your very own Funny Fill-In. Read it out loud for a laugh.

- Want to play by yourself? Just fold over the page and use the cardboard insert at the back as a writing pad. Fill in the blank parts of speech list, and copy your answers into the story.

Fun Fact!

Make sure you check out the amazing **Fun Facts** that appear on every page!

Parts of Speech

To play the game, you'll need to know how to form sentences. This list with examples of the parts of speech and other terms will help you get started:

Noun: The name of a person, place, thing, or idea
Examples: tree, mouth, creature
*The **ocean** is full of colorful **fish**.*

Adjective: A word that describes a noun or pronoun
Examples: green, lazy, friendly
*My **silly** dog won't stop laughing!*

Verb: An action word. In the present tense, a verb often ends in –s or –ing. If the space asks for past tense, changing the vowel or adding a –d or –ed to the end usually will set the sentence in the past.
Examples: swim, hide, plays, running (present tense); biked, rode, jumped (past tense)
*The giraffe **skips** across the savanna.*
*The flower **opened** after the rain.*

Adverb: A word that describes a verb and usually ends in –ly
Examples: quickly, lazily, soundlessly
*Kelley **greedily** ate all the carrots.*

Plural: More than one
Examples: mice, telephones, wrenches
*Why are all the **doors** closing?*

Silly Word or Exclamation: A funny sound, a made-up word, a word you think is totally weird, or a noise someone or something might make
Examples: Ouch! No way! Foozleduzzle! Yikes!
*"**Darn!**" shouted Jim. "These cupcakes are sour!"*

Specific Words: There are many more ways to make your story hilarious. When asked for something like a number, animal, or body part, write in something you think is especially funny.

friend's name

silly word

noun, plural

verb ending in –s

large number

adjective

noun, plural

adjective

liquid

exclamation

noun

same liquid

noun, plural

adjective

same friend's name

verb ending in –ing

verb

animal

verb ending in –ing

 Fun Fact!

A PERSON WHO EXPLORES CAVES IS CALLED A SPELUNKER.

4

Creepy Cave

It's so cool that _____ and I are partners for our class science project! Today we're
                        friend's name

hiking through _____ National Park to take photos of _____ and write about
                 silly word   *noun, plural*

what _____ here. So far we have _____ pictures of the dirt path and one
      verb ending in –s   *large number*

_____ photo of some _____. We're deep in the woods when _____
   adjective   *noun, plural*   *adjective*

clouds form above and _____ begins to pour from the sky. "_____!" I shout. We
                         liquid   *exclamation*

look around for a(n) _____ to wait out the storm. Just then, _____ washes
                       noun   *same liquid*

away _____ covering the opening to a cave. We go inside to dry off, but something feels
       noun, plural

_____ in here. "Shh, do you hear that?" _____ asks. We listen to an odd
  adjective   *same friend's name*

_____ sound coming from the shadows. I _____ around and hope it's just
  verb ending in –ing   *verb*

a(n) _____ _____.
       animal   *verb ending in –ing*

friend's name

noun, plural

adjective

adjective

animal

verb ending in –ing

electronic gadget

noun, plural

a profession

verb

historical figure

sea animal

noun

piece of furniture

same friend's name

clothing item

verb ending in –s

CAVE DRAWINGS
OF HANDS FOUND IN SPAIN ARE MORE THAN 40,000 YEARS OLD.

_____ and I hold our _____ and listen to the _____
 (friend's name)   (noun, plural)   (adjective)

noise in the dimly lit cave. I look down at the _____ rock we're sitting on and see a drawing
                                                 (adjective)

of a fuzzy _____ _____. How odd, I think. I click on my _____
            (animal)   (verb ending in –ing)   (electronic gadget)

and shine it on the surrounding _____. Whoa, there are drawings all over the place!
                                 (noun, plural)

A(n) _____ must have done these! When I _____ closer to check out a drawing
     (a profession)   (verb)

of _____ riding a(n) _____, the noise gets louder and closer.
   (historical figure)   (sea animal)

Suddenly, a troll appears from the shadows holding a(n) _____ and dragging a heavy
                                                        (noun)

_____ behind him. _____ and I scream and grab each
 (piece of furniture)   (same friend's name)

other's _____. The troll _____ up and down and exclaims, "Yay!
         (clothing item)   (verb ending in –s)

I'm happy you're as excited about my art gallery as I am!"

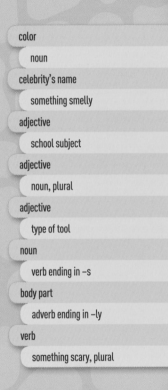

- color
  - noun
- celebrity's name
  - something smelly
- adjective
  - school subject
- adjective
  - noun, plural
- adjective
  - type of tool
- noun
  - verb ending in –s
- body part
  - adverb ending in –ly
- verb
  - something scary, plural

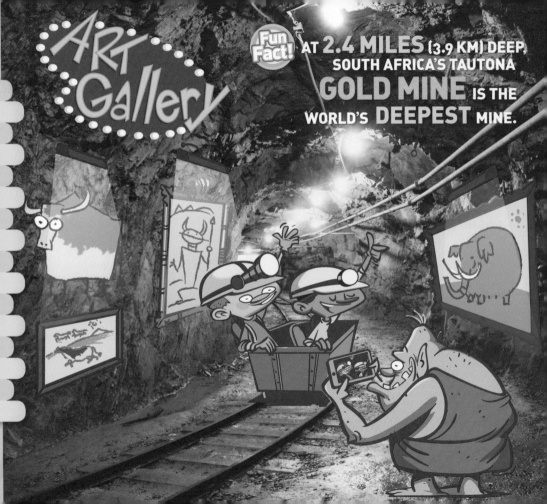

Art Gallery

Fun Fact! AT **2.4 MILES** (3.9 KM) DEEP, SOUTH AFRICA'S TAUTONA **GOLD MINE** IS THE WORLD'S **DEEPEST** MINE.

Troll Tracks

The troll pushes a(n) _____ button on the wall and a(n) _____ lights up that says
                            color   noun

" _____ 's Gallery of _____ Art." He tells us that these are all
      celebrity's name   something smelly

_____ artworks that show the _____ research he has done deep in the cave.
   adjective   school subject

He's now retired and runs this gallery to keep _____ . But since it's so hidden, he doesn't get a
                                                    adjective

lot of _____ . I bet! He offers to take a photo of us in the _____ mining cart he
        noun, plural   adjective

used for his research. We jump in and hold up his mining _____ . The troll steps back to get
                                                              type of tool

the _____ in the photo and accidentally _____ on the release lever. Luckily, I
      noun   verb ending in –s

catch the camera as it flies out of his _____ , but the mining cart is _____ rolling
                                          body part   adverb ending in –ly

down the tracks into the cave! The troll yells after us, " _____ away from the—" We're gone
                                                              verb

before we hear the rest. I hope he wasn't going to say " _____ "!
                                                          something scary, plural

9

body part, plural

verb

adjective

direction

verb

noun

favorite roller coaster

verb ending in –ing

silly word

adjective

same silly word

friend's name

verb ending in –s

body part

adverb ending in –ly

favorite color

Into the Darkness

We grip the mining cart tightly with our _____ (body part, plural) as it zooms deeper into the cave.

I _____ (verb), bracing myself against the _____ (adjective) air hitting my face. The cart turns

_____ (direction), then makes a sharp right. We ride upward, then _____ (verb) down and spin into

a(n) _____ (noun). Wow, this is just like riding the _____ (favorite roller coaster)! Too bad we can't see

where we're _____ (verb ending in –ing). "_____ (silly word)!" I shout. My voice echoes back, followed by

a(n) _____ (adjective) echo from somewhere in the cave. "_____ (same silly word)!" we hear over and over.

Then _____ (friend's name) and I hear laughing. Who or what is laughing? "What's so funny?" I shout.

"You!" the voice _____ (verb ending in –s) back. I feel something brush past my _____ (body part) and land

_____ (adverb ending in –ly) in the cart with us. We turn around and see a creature with _____ (favorite color)

glowing eyes staring back at us. It's my favorite color, but it definitely doesn't look good now!

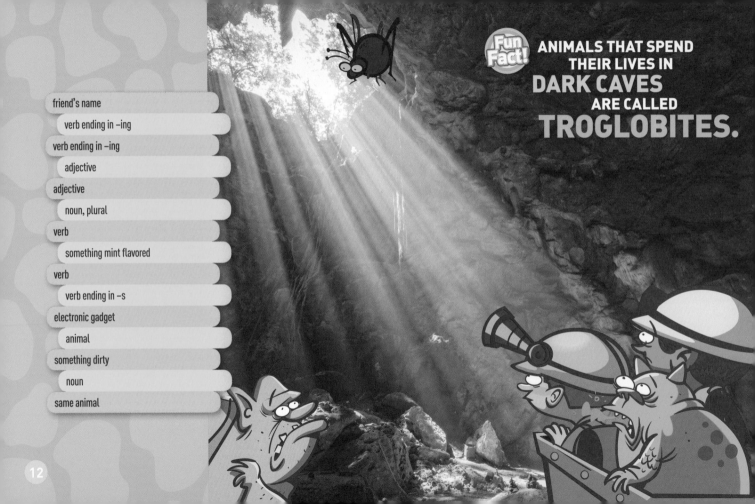

friend's name

    verb ending in –ing

verb ending in –ing

    adjective

adjective

    noun, plural

verb

    something mint flavored

verb

    verb ending in –s

electronic gadget

    animal

something dirty

    noun

same animal

Fun Fact! ANIMALS THAT SPEND THEIR LIVES IN **DARK CAVES** ARE CALLED **TROGLOBITES.**

12

Goofy Guest

_____ and I are _____ out! I can't decide what's scarier: _____
 friend's name   verb ending in –ing   verb ending in –ing

backward into a(n) _____ cave or the creature with _____ eyes staring at us.
                              adjective   adjective

Just when we are wishing we could grow _____ and _____ away from here, the
                                                           noun, plural   verb

mysterious creature burps. What a stink! Has this thing never heard of _____ ?
                                                                                    something mint flavored

"We should at least see what's about to _____ us," I whisper. My hand _____
                                                       verb   verb ending in –s

as I switch on my _____ . We're stunned. The creature is a cute _____ ! But
                          electronic gadget   animal

boy, its breath smells like _____ . "I've been waiting for a(n) _____ out of
                                  something dirty   noun

here," the _____ says. Ahead we see light streaming through a sinkhole in the top of the
                 same animal

cave. A shadowy figure sits in the corner. With one creature above and one in the cart, we're not sure this

ride could get any crazier. Boy, were we wrong.

- friend's name
  - adjective
- something sharp, plural
  - adjective
- verb
  - noun
- lucky number
  - adjective
- same friend's name
  - verb
- adjective
  - something sticky
- verb ending in −s
  - adverb ending in −ly

Fun Fact! WEAVERS IN MADAGASCAR CREATED A RARE TAPESTRY MADE ENTIRELY OF SPIDER SILK.

Rappelling Rescue

"Let's keep this ride moving!" _____ says. But with the extra weight in the cart, we
                                    friend's name

come to a stop high above the ground. Suddenly, the shadow of a creature with _____ legs and
                                                                                   adjective

two _____ appears above us. Something _____ and wet hits my face. Creature
      something sharp, plural   adjective

drool! It's hungry, and we're dinner—a la carte! Maybe we can _____ down to the cave floor. I
                                                                   verb

toss a(n) _____ to gauge how high up we are. We listen for _____ minutes
             noun   lucky number

before we hear it hit the bottom. Uh oh. The creature gets right in our faces and says, "Need some help?"

Whew! It's a(n) _____ spider! _____ and I use the spider's silk to rappel to
                   adjective   same friend's name

the cave floor and _____. The silk is _____ and feels like _____.
                      verb   adjective   something sticky

"All fixed!" the spider shouts from above as it _____ down after us and _____
                                                   verb ending in –s   adverb ending in –ly

lands beside us on the cave floor. Our hero!

friend's name

sport

adjective

number

favorite board game

type of dessert

same friend's name

body part

something noisy

adjective

animal, plural

small number

sea creature, plural

adjective

noun, plural

something fast

body part

Fun Fact!

AT THE **BATHTUB REGATTA** IN BELGIUM, PARTICIPANTS RACE IN **BATHTUBS** AND OTHER HOMEMADE FLOATS.

FINISH

Our new friend the giant spider asks _____ and me to join his _____ team
friend's name   sport

in a(n) _____ race. But the rules are really strange: We have to play _____ rounds
adjective   number

of _____ while paddling across an underground lake. Piece of _____ !
favorite board game   type of dessert

Our boat is tiny, so I have to sit on _____ 's _____ . A(n) _____
same friend's name   body part   something noisy

toots and it's a(n) _____ dash to the finish line! A boat with albino _____ pulls
adjective   animal, plural

into the lead. Then we're passed by _____ blind _____ riding in a
small number   sea creature, plural

submarine. That seems a little _____ . But then I realize our team easily has more legs and
adjective

_____ than the competition. We paddle like a(n) _____ and sail
noun, plural   something fast

through the finish line to take first place! Now that's putting your best _____
body part

forward! Ahead, we see a cavern with flashing lights.

adjective

    friend's name

verb ending in –s

    verb ending in –s

same friend's name

    musical instrument

adjective

    type of rock

horn instrument

    musical instrument

noun, plural

    fictional character

adjective ending in –est

    favorite song

exclamation

    verb

same friend's name

    noun, plural

Fun Fact!

THE GREAT STALACPIPE ORGAN, IN LURAY CAVERNS, VIRGINIA, U.S.A., IS THE WORLD'S **LARGEST MUSICAL INSTRUMENT.**

The Original Rock Band

A large crowd is gathering and lights are flashing outside a(n) _____ cavern. _____ and I decide to
adjective   friend's name

check out the action. As we step inside, a rock band bursts into song. Everyone _____ and _____
verb ending in –s   verb ending in –s

to the beat. _____ and I are extra excited because we both play the _____ in our school
same friend's name   musical instrument

band. But this concert is unlike anything we've ever seen. All the instruments are made of _____
adjective

minerals from the cave itself. There's a(n) _____ guitar and a copper _____. Plus, a huge
type of rock   horn instrument

_____ is carved directly into the cave wall, and it vibrates the _____ all around us.
musical instrument   noun, plural

We dance like we're _____ while the band plays the _____ metal songs of all time.
fictional character   adjective ending in –est

"Play '_____'!" I shout, but the singer doesn't know it. "_____!" I cry, jumping onstage with
favorite song   exclamation

the band and grabbing a microphone. I _____ out the lyrics while _____ drums on a set
verb   same friend's name

of steel _____. This must be where rock and roll got started!
noun, plural

friend's name

pop star

verb ending in –ing

noun, plural

adjective

type of dance

gymnastic move, plural

adjective ending in –er

shape

animal

adjective

relative's name

barnyard animal

past-tense verb

somewhere smelly

same friend's name

verb

body part, plural

adjective

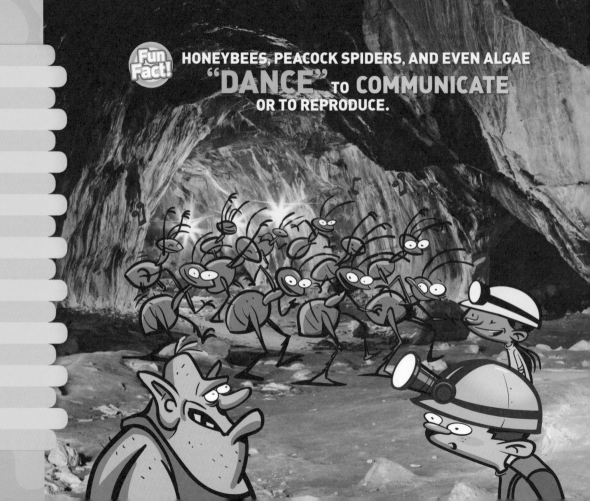

Fun Fact! HONEYBEES, PEACOCK SPIDERS, AND EVEN ALGAE "DANCE" TO COMMUNICATE OR TO REPRODUCE.

Flash Mob!

_____ (friend's name) and I are rocking on stage like we're _____ (pop star)! We look at the cheering crowd and see tons of ants _____ (verb ending in –ing) into the concert hall. All at once, they look at their _____ (noun, plural) and break into a synchronized dance. It's a flash mob! These ants are _____ (adjective) dancers. They know _____ (type of dance) and can even do _____ (gymnastic move, plural) without missing a beat. It gets _____ (adjective ending in –er) when they climb on each other to build a super _____ (shape). Together they look like a giant _____ (animal) dancing the cha-cha! I haven't seen a performance this _____ (adjective) since _____ (relative's name) tripped on the family _____ (barnyard animal) and they both _____ (past-tense verb) into the _____ (somewhere smelly). _____ (same friend's name) and I slide into line with the ants. First we wiggle to the left, next we _____ (verb) our big toes, and then we hop on the tip of our _____ (body part, plural). I can't wait to teach the dance to everyone at school. This is sure to be the next _____ (adjective) trend!

- friend's name
  - adjective
- verb
  - beverage
- type of building
  - noun
- type of important person
  - large number
- adjective
  - noun
- large animal, plural
  - favorite video game
- animal, plural
  - type of transportation, plural
- verb ending in –ing
  - verb ending in –s
- favorite snack

Fun Fact! A GROUP OF **ANTS** BUILT A **SUPERCOLONY** THAT SPANS 3,700 MILES (6,000 KM).

Sisterhood of the Traveling Ants

Trying to keep up with dancing ants makes _____ and me really _____ .
                                        friend's name   adjective

Fortunately, the ants _____ us back to their colony for _____ and a snack. But first
                         verb   beverage

they insist on giving us a tour of their underground _____ . Wow, this place is a(n)
                                                     type of building

_____ fit for a(n) _____ . There are _____ levels, with everything
     noun   type of important person   large number

you could need or want. The ants show us the theater that only plays _____ movies. There's a
                                                                      adjective

bouncy _____ that fits up to six _____ . Next to that is the arcade, where you can
          noun   large animal, plural

play _____ starting on any level you want. The ants even have an aquarium full of
     favorite video game

undiscovered sea _____ . My favorite room, though, is the bumper _____
                  animal, plural   type of transportation, plural

arena. We ride around, _____ into each other until my stomach _____ .
                        verb ending in –ing   verb ending in –s

The ants offer us some mold to eat, but we politely decline. We'd rather find _____ !
                                                                               favorite snack

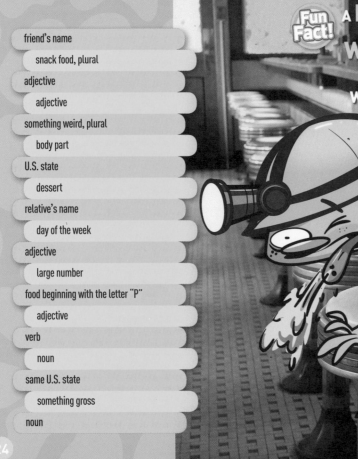

- friend's name
  - snack food, plural
- adjective
  - adjective
- something weird, plural
  - body part
- U.S. state
  - dessert
- relative's name
  - day of the week
- adjective
  - large number
- food beginning with the letter "P"
  - adjective
- verb
  - noun
- same U.S. state
  - something gross
- noun

It's been hours since _____ (friend's name) and I ate our _____ (snack food, plural) back in the woods.

Thankfully, we find an underground diner packed with customers. This place must be _____ (adjective)!

The menu has a lot of _____ (adjective) choices, like leafy salads and all-natural _____ (something weird, plural). But

what really catches my _____ (body part) is the _____ (U.S. state) mud pie. The photo of it looks like my

favorite chocolate _____ (dessert) that _____ (relative's name) makes every _____ (day of the week). I'm so

_____ (adjective) to eat the pie that I ask for _____ (large number) orders of it. But just in case that's not enough, I

order a side of dirty _____ (food beginning with the letter "P"). When the dishes arrive, they look even more _____ (adjective)

than they do in the menu pictures. I can't wait to _____ (verb) in! I scoop a large _____ (noun)-ful of

the _____ (same U.S. state) mud pie into my mouth. It tastes like a(n) _____ (something gross). We spit everything

out and wipe our tongues on the _____ (noun). What a dirty surprise!

- friend's name
  - noun, plural
- verb ending in –ing
  - adjective ending in –est
- adjective
  - small number
- color
  - animal
- adjective
  - body part, plural
- verb ending in –s
  - noun, plural
- verb
  - cartoon character
- verb
  - same friend's name
- famous athlete
  - verb
- adjective ending in –est

_____ and I run into a group of odd-looking creatures that are sawing _____
friend's name   _noun, plural_

and _____ clay. They are definitely the _____ bunch down here. Each
verb ending in –ing   _adjective ending in –est_

one has a(n) _____ body with _____ toe(s), a long _____ tail, and
adjective   _small number_   _color_

a giant head like a(n) _____ . We're surprised that they are so _____ at sculpting
animal   _adjective_

because they don't have any eyes. Instead, they use their _____ to feel how something
body part, plural

_____ . We ask them to teach us how they create the beautiful _____ . First,
verb ending in –s   _noun, plural_

one will _____ like _____ while the others _____ . Then they switch
verb   _cartoon character_   _verb_

places. _____ and I pose like _____ and ask them if they'll
same friend's name   _famous athlete_

carve a sculpture of us. They _____ with excitement and say, "Of course! You two are by far
verb

the _____ things in this cave!"
adjective ending in –est

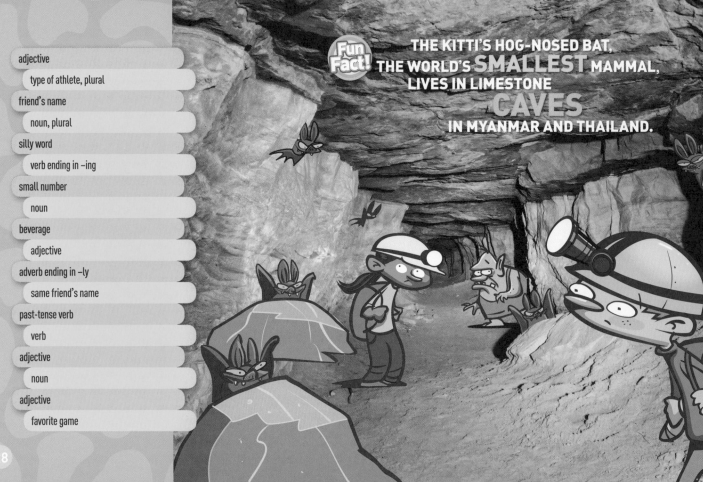

adjective
type of athlete, plural
friend's name
noun, plural
silly word
verb ending in –ing
small number
noun
beverage
adjective
adverb ending in –ly
same friend's name
past-tense verb
verb
adjective
noun
adjective
favorite game

Fun Fact! THE KITTI'S HOG-NOSED BAT, THE WORLD'S SMALLEST MAMMAL, LIVES IN LIMESTONE CAVES IN MYANMAR AND THAILAND.

We're deep in the cave when suddenly a couple of _____ bats swoop overhead like aerial
_____ . "Duck!" _____ shouts. We soon discover they're competing in a series

(adjective)

(type of athlete, plural) *(friend's name)*

of _____ . It's like field day at school, except down here it's called _____ Day.

(noun, plural) *(silly word)*

The bats challenge us to the next event: ringtoss. Luckily, I've been practicing my _____ skills since

(verb ending in –ing)

I was _____ . Did I mention I also have an excellent sense of _____ ? As for the bats,

(small number) *(noun)*

well, let's just say ringtoss is not their cup of _____ . Their wingspans are too _____ ,

(beverage) *(adjective)*

and they can't even throw _____ . _____ and I win this event, but the bats

(adverb ending in –ly) *(same friend's name)*

_____ us in the next event: hide-and-_____ . Not only did they already know all

(past-tense verb) *(verb)*

the _____ spots, they could hear us crawling into a hiding _____ . It's a tie game when

(adjective) *(noun)*

we all agree to join together in a(n) _____ game of _____ instead.

(adjective) *(favorite game)*

29

body part

   adjective

friend's name

   verb

pattern

   animal

number

   exotic location

adjective

   large number

adverb ending in –ly

   something gooey

type of chore

   adjective

verb

   clothing item, plural

liquid

   type of swim

Fun Fact! "SODA STRAWS" AND "BACON STRIPS" ARE NAMES FOR STALACTITE FORMATIONS.

Tubular Tour

I wipe the sweat off my _____ . Exploring caves is _____ work! We arrive at an
                        body part   adjective

underground river, and _____ suggests we join a river tour. So I _____ into a(n)
                        friend's name   verb

_____ inner tube in the shape of a(n) _____ and link it up to the rest of the group. Our
pattern   animal

guide is a(n) _____-headed reptile named _____ . She is _____ and knows
              number   exotic location   adjective

everything about the cave's formations and history. The area we're floating through is _____ years old
                                                                                        large number

and _____ formed when _____ repeatedly washed the rock away. And I thought
    adverb ending in –ly   something gooey

_____ took forever to do! We see _____ stalactites hanging from the ceiling, and our
type of chore   adjective

tubes _____ around stalagmites rising from the ground. The river picks up speed as we get near
      verb

the end of the tour. We unhook our inner tubes, put on our _____ , and tumble over a(n)
                                                            clothing item, plural

_____-fall. Look out below, here comes my famous _____ !
liquid   type of swim

31

friend's name

    something smelly

adjective

    adjective

favorite color

    spicy food

adjective

    verb ending in –ing

same friend's name

    noun, plural

relative's name

    verb ending in –s

animal

    something gross, plural

noun, plural

    body part, plural

adjective

    same color

Fun Fact! THE TOWN OF ROTORUA, NEW ZEALAND, SMELLS LIKE **ROTTEN EGGS** DUE TO **SULPHUR** IN THE AREA.

"Phew. What a stink!" _____ exclaims as we arrive at the shore. There's a sign
friend's name

saying "_____ Springs." It's famous for its rocky shore and _____ water. The
something smelly   adjective

geothermal activity of a(n) _____ volcano makes the water seem to glow shades of _____ .
adjective   favorite color

And the water is so warm I feel like a(n) _____ just dipping in my _____ toe.
spicy food   adjective

Instead of _____ , _____ and I want to put our _____ up and relax.
verb ending in –ing   same friend's name   noun, plural

It's hard to relax though, when the air smells like _____ 's feet after (s)he _____
relative's name   verb ending in –s

a marathon. We wave down a(n) _____ who is selling nose plugs and large _____
animal   something gross, plural

on a stick. After putting on the nose plugs, we wrap _____ around our _____
noun, plural   body part, plural

and enjoy the steam of the _____ water. Time to get out of the water and continue our journey,
adjective

though. I hope this doesn't leave a(n) _____ glow on my skin.
same color

first name beginning with "W"

word beginning with "R"

a profession

animal that lives underground

clothing item

noun

something gross

your hometown

verb ending in –ing

past-tense verb

verb

adjective

noun

something used for travel

noun

something old

pet's name

Fun Fact!

NEW YORK CITY'S FIRST SUBWAY USED A GIANT FAN TO MOVE A CAR FORWARD AND BACKWARD.

I'm starting to wonder how we'll find our way out of this cave when I hear a *whoosh!* It's the sound of the cave's under-

ground subway, the WORTS. WORTS stands for _____'s Obviously _____

first name beginning with "W"   word beginning with "R"

Transportation System. It was named after its inventor: a hairy _____ _____

a profession   animal that lives underground

who was always in a hurry. We squeeze onboard next to a tall rat wearing a(n) _____ and carrying a

clothing item

miniature _____ . "Are you going to work?" we ask the rat. "Yes, I'm a professional _____

noun   something gross

taste-tester in _____'s finest restaurant. When he asks why we're _____ down

your hometown   verb ending in –ing

here, I realize we totally _____ our science project! The rat suggests we _____

past-tense verb   verb

in an archaeological dig happening right now on the _____ side of the _____ . He

adjective   noun

pulls a(n) _____ out of his _____ to help us get there. He also hands us

something used for travel   noun

a(n) _____ to help pay the WORTS fare. I wish _____ was as well behaved as this rodent!

something old   pet's name

- friend's name
- shape
- adverb ending in –ly
- body part, plural
- kitchen utensil, plural
- verb ending in –ing
- same friend's name
- something slimy
- something enormous
- silly word
- same friend's name
- past-tense verb
- toy
- animal
- adjective
- something sticky
- noun, plural
- country

Fun Fact! THE **DINOSAUR** *VECTIDRACO DAISYMORRISAE* IS NAMED AFTER DAISY MORRIS, ITS **FOUR-YEAR-OLD** DISCOVERER.

_____ and I arrive at an archaeological site and the excavation crew immediately
friend's name

gives us the lowdown. They've roped off a(n) _____-shaped site and are _____
shape   *adverb ending in –ly*

mapping every bit of it. So far, they've found several dinosaur _____ and even a few petrified
body part, plural

_____ . We each pick up a tool for _____ artifacts. _____
kitchen utensil, plural   *verb ending in –ing*   *same friend's name*

uses a long _____ , while I carefully scrape the soil away with a scratchy _____ .
something slimy   *something enormous*

"_____ !" _____ shouts. "Look what I _____ !" (S)he holds
silly word   *same friend's name*   *past-tense verb*

up an ancient _____ . I uncover an inflatable _____ . It doesn't look old or very
toy   *animal*

interesting, so I dig farther until something _____ catches my eye. I change tools and use
adjective

_____ to remove all the _____ around my find. Whoa,
something sticky   *noun, plural*

it looks like a diamond the size of _____ !
country

- adjective
  - friend's name
- adjective
  - adjective
- jewelry, plural
  - clothing item
- your birthstone
  - verb
- noun
  - adjective
- adjective
  - verb
- math teacher's name
  - noun, plural
- royal title
  - adjective

Fun Fact! EARTHWORMS ARE COVERED IN SMALL HAIRS THAT HELP THEM BURROW THROUGH DIRT.

Diamonds Are a Worm's Best Friend

Everyone will be so _____ when they see my diamond discovery! _____
adjective   friend's name

and I take it to a(n) _____ jewelry shop to learn more about it. Earthworms run the shop,
adjective

and they love gemstones, especially diamonds. They're decked out in _____ tiaras and emerald
adjective

_____ . One worm is even wearing a(n) _____ made entirely of _____ .
jewelry, plural   clothing item   your birthstone

I'll have to ask him if I can _____ that for our class _____ next week! Clearly, these
verb   noun

worms have _____ taste, so it's no wonder they're in awe of my _____ find. They
adjective   adjective

measure and study its every angle and edge. Then the worms _____ a giant calculator that would
verb

make _____ really jealous. After running the _____ , they tell me what
math teacher's name   noun, plural

I found is actually a very rare diamond tooth from _____ Rex the Eighth. Not only can we use
royal title

this to ace our next science project, now we'll get _____ points in history class, too!
adjective

famous city
_____

today's date
_____

your name
_____

verb ending in –s
_____

adjective
_____

friend's name
_____

type of head wear, plural
_____

noun, plural
_____

same friend's name
_____

noun
_____

adjective
_____

noun
_____

favorite actor
_____

adjective
_____

verb
_____

celebrity's name
_____

verb
_____

something odd, plural
_____

THE LARGEST
DIAMOND
EVER SOLD AT AUCTION WENT FOR
$30.6 MILLION.

Made for a Museum

When the mayor of underground ＿＿＿＿＿＿ (famous city) hears about my royal tooth, she proclaims ＿＿＿＿＿ (today's date) International ＿＿＿＿＿ (your name) Day! The celebration ＿＿＿＿＿ (verb ending in –s) off with a(n) ＿＿＿＿＿ (adjective) parade, and we're in it! ＿＿＿＿＿ (friend's name) and I wear ＿＿＿＿＿ (type of head wear, plural) and toss ＿＿＿＿＿ (noun, plural) to the crowd. At a special ceremony, the mayor shows ＿＿＿＿＿ (same friend's name) and me a(n) ＿＿＿＿＿ (noun) with both our names on it, and the title "Most ＿＿＿＿＿ (adjective) Explorers in Cave History!" It's in the city's Hall of ＿＿＿＿＿ (noun) between an autographed photo of ＿＿＿＿＿ (favorite actor) and a(n) ＿＿＿＿＿ (adjective) empty space. The mayor points to the space and says, "That's where we'll ＿＿＿＿＿ (verb) the tooth!" What? But how will I become rich and famous like ＿＿＿＿＿ (celebrity's name) if the tooth is way down here? Then I think about what a pain it would be to ＿＿＿＿＿ (verb) it all the way home. We decide to check it out. Besides, it really completes the museum's collection of ＿＿＿＿＿ (something odd, plural).

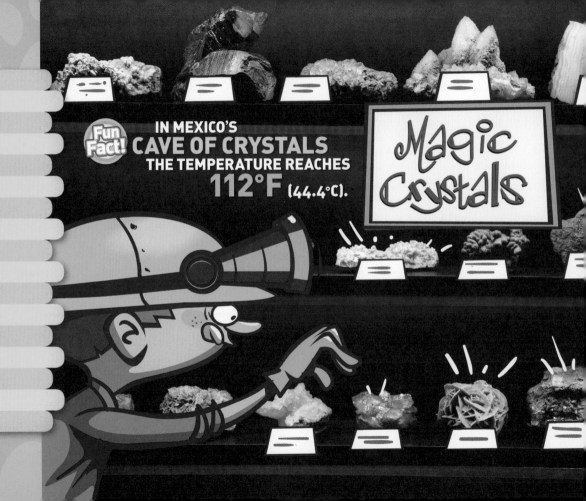

- friend's name
  - verb
- adjective ending in –est
  - adverb ending in –ly
- animal with a tail
  - adjective
- adverb ending in –ly
  - adjective
- body part
  - animal sound
- something expensive
  - noun
- verb
  - same friend's name
- electronic gadget
  - sports equipment, plural
- something silly

Fun Fact!

IN MEXICO'S
CAVE OF CRYSTALS
THE TEMPERATURE REACHES
112°F (44.4°C).

Magic Crystals

Not So Crystal Clear

_____ and I _____ into a room filled with the _____ crystals we've ever seen.
friend's name   verb   adjective ending in –est

I lean in _____ to one and see words written on it. Did a(n) _____ scribble these words
           adverb ending in –ly   animal with a tail

with its tail? Because they look like a(n) _____ mess. Nearby, we see a sign that explains these are magic
                                          adjective

crystals. Each one has special directions on it, and if we follow them _____ we'll be granted a wish.
                                                                         adverb ending in –ly

I quickly read over the _____ text on one crystal and get started. I spin on my _____ and
                        adjective   body part

hold my left foot above my head. Then I _____ like an animal and wish for a(n) _____ .
                                         animal sound   something expensive

Bang! A curly _____ appears on my head and I immediately _____ from its weight.
              noun   verb

_____ tries next and wishes for the newest _____ . Poof! A set of
same friend's name   electronic gadget

_____ appears. Good thing we didn't wish for _____ ! Since we can't
sports equipment, plural   something silly

seem to wish our way out, we're going to have to keep exploring.

- measurement of time, plural
- something cold, plural
- adjective
- noun
- something sweet
- friend's name
- noun, plural
- verb
- type of building
- adjective ending in –er
- favorite flavor
- salty food
- noun, plural
- large number
- good smell
- noun
- verb ending in –s
- noun
- body part

Fun Fact! AN ICE-CREAM SHOP IN VENEZUELA SERVES **850 FLAVORS** —INCLUDING SQUID, MACARONI AND CHEESE, AND ROSE.

TODAY'S SPECIAL: BERRY POTTER

Brrr Cave

We've been walking for _____ , and suddenly it's gotten as cold as _____ .
measurement of time, plural   something cold, plural

The walls are covered in ice. *Brr!* But what's that _____ smell? Do I detect the hint of a(n)
                                                        adjective

_____ covered in _____ ? *Mmm.* _____ and I use his/her _____
noun   something sweet   friend's name   noun, plural

to _____ along the cave's slippery wall. Deep in a corner, we see bears working in an ice-cream
    verb

_____ . If their ice cream smells this good, I'm sure it tastes even _____ . I always
type of building   adjective ending in –er

go with _____ , but the chocolate _____ sounds really yummy. This is going to be
         favorite flavor   salty food

a tough choice! We pull up two _____ to sit on and ask for _____ scoops
                                noun, plural   large number

of _____ . The bear behind the counter grins and scoops the ice cream right from a(n)
    good smell

_____ ! Talk about cool! We watch another bear making milk shakes. It _____ the
noun   verb ending in –s

ice cream in a(n) _____ with its furry _____ . I'm glad we didn't order that.
                  noun   body part

adjective

verb

friend's name

noun

adjective

local sports team

verb

adverb ending in –ly

number

noun

body part

type of transportation

verb

same type of transportation

plant

Resurfacing

We've had a(n) _____ time exploring underground. But it's time to go home. We walk and
              adjective

walk ... but which way did we _____ in? _____ and I can't even remember how long
                              verb   friend's name

we've been down here. I knock on a nearby _____ and a(n) _____ mole wearing
                                          noun   adjective

a(n) _____ jersey answers. What luck! She says she can _____ us the way home.
     local sports team   verb

She begins to dig _____ through the soil, but she's not making much of a dent. At this rate,
                  adverb ending in –ly

it will take _____ years to get home. "Do you want a(n) _____ to help dig that tunnel to
             number   noun

the surface?" I ask her. "I'm not digging a tunnel," she says, shaking her _____ . "I was looking for
                                                                          body part

my _____ keys." She holds them up, and we all _____ into her _____ .
   type of transportation   verb   same type of transportation

In minutes, we pop up in the _____ garden in front of my house. With all the photos and
                             plant

stories from our journey, I know our science project is going to rock!

How to Play Funny Fill-In!

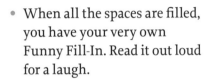

Love to create amazing stories? Good, because this one stars YOU. Get ready to laugh with all your friends—you can play with as many people as you want! Make sure to keep this book on your shelf. You'll want to read it again and again!

Are You Ready to Laugh?

- One person picks a story—you can start at the beginning, the middle, or the end of the book.

- Ask a friend to call out a word that the space asks for—noun, verb, or something else—and write it in the blank space. If there's more than one player, ask the next person to say a word. Extra points for creativity!

- When all the spaces are filled, you have your very own Funny Fill-In. Read it out loud for a laugh.

- Want to play by yourself? Just fold over the page and use the cardboard insert at the back as a writing pad. Fill in the blank parts of speech list, and copy your answers into the story.

Make sure you check out the amazing **Fun Facts** that appear on every page!

Parts of Speech

To play the game, you'll need to know how to form sentences. This list with examples of the parts of speech and other terms will help you get started:

Noun: The name of a person, place, thing, or idea
Examples: tree, mouth, creature
*The **ocean** is full of colorful **fish**.*

Adjective: A word that describes a noun or pronoun
Examples: green, lazy, friendly
*My **silly** dog won't stop laughing!*

Verb: An action word. In the present tense, a verb often ends in –s or –ing. If the space asks for past tense, changing the vowel or adding a –d or –ed to the end usually will set the sentence in the past.
Examples: swim, hide, plays, running (present tense); biked, rode, jumped (past tense)
*The giraffe **skips** across the savanna.*
*The flower **opened** after the rain.*

Adverb: A word that describes a verb and usually ends in –ly
Examples: quickly, lazily, soundlessly
*Kelley **greedily** ate all the carrots.*

Plural: More than one
Examples: mice, telephones, wrenches
*Why are all the **doors** closing?*

Silly Word or Exclamation: A funny sound, a made-up word, a word you think is totally weird, or a noise someone or something might make
Examples: Ouch! No way! Foozleduzzle! Yikes!
*"**Darn!**" shouted Jim. "These cupcakes are sour!"*

Specific Words: There are many more ways to make your story hilarious. When asked for something like a number, animal, or body part, write in something you think is especially funny.

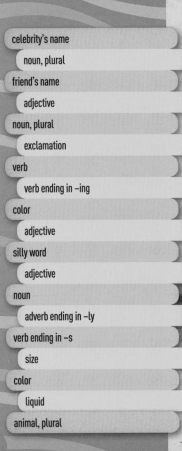

- celebrity's name
  - noun, plural
- friend's name
  - adjective
- noun, plural
  - exclamation
- verb
  - verb ending in –ing
- color
  - adjective
- silly word
  - adjective
- noun
  - adverb ending in –ly
- verb ending in –s
  - size
- color
  - liquid
- animal, plural

Fun Fact! MORE WATER IS IN THE PACIFIC OCEAN THAN IN ALL THE OTHER SEAS AND OCEANS COMBINED.

PRESS ME

All Aboard!

It's a beautiful day at _____ beach. My parents are asleep in their
  celebrity's name

_____, so _____ and I go for a walk away from the crowds.
  noun, plural   _friend's name_

We spot a(n) _____ boat that washed ashore not far from our _____.
  adjective   _noun, plural_

"_____!" I shout. Together, we _____ toward the waves, _____
  exclamation   _verb_   _verb ending in –ing_

in to explore. The boat is painted _____ and has something written in big, bold letters
  color

on its side: "The _____ _____." That's not all. A(n) _____
  adjective   _silly word_   _adjective_

_____ at the front reads: "PRESS ME." Before I can say anything, my friend
  noun

_____ _____ it. Suddenly, we find ourselves in a(n) _____
  adverb ending in –ly _verb ending in –s_   _size_

submarine, surrounded by _____ _____ and striped _____.
                           color   _liquid_   _animal, plural_

And bubbles. Lots and lots of bubbles. Anchors aweigh!

- verb ending in –ing
- noun
- adjective
- clothing item, plural
- friend's name
- adjective
- land animal
- water animal
- large number
- body part, plural
- color
- teacher's name
- verb ending in –s
- noun
- verb ending in –s
- adjective
- noun
- same friend's name

Fun Fact! AN OCTOPUS CAN HAVE NEARLY 2,000 SUCKERS ON ITS ARMS.

In our first hour on the submarine, we decide to go scuba _____ (verb ending in –ing) . We jump

into the _____ (noun) wearing _____ (adjective) _____ (clothing item, plural) . Underwater, we see

all kinds of awesome things. I swim ahead of _____ (friend's name) —and come face-to-face

with a(n) _____ (adjective) creature with the head of a(n) _____ (land animal) and the body of a(n)

_____ (water animal) ! It has _____ (large number) _____ (body part, plural) covered in _____ (color) stripes.

"Hi," the creature says politely. "My name is _____ (teacher's name) . Nice to meet you." Then it

_____ (verb ending in –s) onto a(n) _____ (noun) and _____ (verb ending in –s) at me. I turn around

to get my friend's attention. By the time (s)he catches up, the creature is gone—it swam faster than

a(n) _____ (adjective) _____ (noun) ! _____ (same friend's name) doesn't believe my story,

but that's OK. I may have discovered a new species!

- verb ending in –ing
  - noun
- animal
  - body part, plural
- noun, plural
  - large number
- animal, plural
  - adverb ending in –ly
- kind of fish, plural
  - something slimy
- song title
  - foreign language
- clothing item
  - adjective
- animal
  - noun
- animal noise
  - exclamation
- movie title

DETACHED **SEA STAR ARMS** SOMETIMES GROW **NEW BODIES.**

SEA STAR TALENT SHOW

We're _____ along the ocean floor when we hear a roar of applause. We see a sign
          verb ending in –ing

hanging over a(n) _____ in the sand. Under the sign, a(n) _____ is using
                    noun   animal

its _____ to juggle _____ . It's an undersea talent show! We stop to
    body part, plural   noun, plural

watch the rest of the acts with the audience. Next, _____ polka-dotted _____
                                                      large number   animal, plural

dance _____ . A school of _____ tell jokes. A(n) _____
       adverb ending in –ly   kind of fish, plural   something slimy

sings "_____" in _____ . Then a sea turtle wearing a(n)
        song title   foreign language

_____ makes a(n) _____ _____ disappear in a cloud of _____ .
 clothing item   adjective   animal   noun

Seconds later, following a(n) _____ , the sea turtle disappears too. "_____ !"
                               animal noise   exclamation

we shout, clapping wildly. Who knew sea turtles knew magic? I close the show by acting out my favorite

scene from _____ . The sea turtle won, but I still had a blast.
            movie title

large number

   adjective

color

   animal body part, plural

celebrity's name

   verb

clothing item

   animal

favorite book

   vegetable

body part, plural

   verb ending in –ing

animal body part

   type of job

noun

   favorite food, plural

favorite dessert

 SCIENTISTS KNOW MORE ABOUT THE **SURFACE OF THE MOON** THAN THEY KNOW ABOUT THE **BOTTOM OF THE OCEAN.**

Welcome to Mermaid-ville

Our submarine speeds along at _____ miles an hour, and we spot something _____ in
_____(large number)_____   ___(adjective)___

the distance. Underwater skyscrapers! Or are they called seascrapers here? "Welcome to Mermaid-ville," says

a woman with _____ _____ . "My name is _____ .
____(color)____   ___(animal body part, plural)___   ___(celebrity's name)___

Would you like a tour?" Of course, we do! We _____ onto the giant stingray she is riding and take off.
____(verb)____

First, we go to see the school—where the principal is a(n) _____-wearing _____ !
_____(clothing item)_____   ___(animal)___

At the library we see mermaids reading _____ and sipping _____-flavored
_____(favorite book)_____   ___(vegetable)___

coffee. Our tour guide hears our _____ _____—it's been awhile since
_____(body part, plural)_____   ___(verb ending in –ing)___

we last ate. She takes us to a diner called _____'s Place. We park the stingray outside and follow
_____(animal body part)_____

a(n) _____ to our _____ , where we order lots of sea salt–covered _____ .
___(type of job)___   __(noun)__   ___(favorite food, plural)___

Our new mermaid friend even treats us to _____ . What a great city!
_____(favorite dessert)_____

11

- friend's name
  - noun
- verb
  - noun
- adjective
  - clothing item, plural
- famous sporting event
  - type of job
- animal, plural
  - verb ending in –ing
- color
  - adverb ending in –ly
- animal, plural
  - same color
- noun
  - verb
- silly word
  - adjective

Fun Fact! SEAHORSES CAN LOOK IN TWO DIFFERENT DIRECTIONS AT ONCE.

After we say goodbye to the mermaids, _____ and I swim past a(n) _____ .
friend's name   noun

It looks like there is a horse race taking place. And not just any horse race—a seahorse race! We both

_____ a _____ and go inside to watch. Everyone is wearing _____
verb   noun   adjective

_____ , just like at the _____ . A lobster _____ lists
clothing item, plural   famous sporting event   type of job

the names of the contenders. The _____ are _____ on the _____
animal, plural   verb ending in –ing   color

-spotted seahorse to win _____ , but the _____ think the returning
adverb ending in –ly   animal, plural

champion will take it. The race is a close one. At the last minute, the _____ -striped seahorse
same color

pulls ahead to win. Afterward, everyone lines up to take their _____ on the seahorses.
noun

I _____ up onto the winner, while my friend sits on another one. The lobster says,
verb

"Say _____ !" Not that we need a picture to remember this _____ moment.
silly word   adjective

- noun
  - noun
- body part, plural
  - liquid
- electronic gadget
  - exotic destination
- verb ending in –ing
  - verb ending in –ing
- adjective
  - animal
- food
  - famous landmark
- noun
  - noun
- friend's name
  - large number
- noun
  - noun
- noun, plural

Fun Fact! THE WORLD'S **TALLEST** SANDCASTLE WAS BUILT WITH **1.6 MILLION** POUNDS (726 METRIC TONS) OF SAND!

14

King of the Sandcastle

We've seen a lot of cool things underwater, but we miss the feel of the warm _____ (noun) and the

_____ (noun) under our _____ (body part, plural). Our vehicle pops out above the deep _____ (liquid). Using

a(n) _____ (electronic gadget), we spot the beautiful _____ (exotic destination). Aloha!

After _____ (verb ending in –ing) onshore, we see signs for a sandcastle contest and decide to enter. Locals and

tourists are _____ (verb ending in –ing) all kinds of _____ (adjective) things out of sand everywhere

you look. We spot a sand _____ (animal), a sand _____ (food), and even a sand _____ (famous landmark).

People are using things like _____ (noun) and _____ (noun) to make their creations stand

out. _____ (friend's name) enters us in the contest, and we build a(n) _____ (large number)-foot-tall sand

_____ (noun), complete with a sand _____ (noun). We win the big prize—_____ (noun, plural)

for two to a luau that night!

ocean animal

    adjective

number

    adjective

direction

    body part, plural

verb

    royal title

country name

    friend's name

verb ending in –s

    animal, plural

verb ending in –ing

    body part, plural

same ocean animal

    animal body part

adjective ending in –est

Fun Fact! THRILL-SEEKING TOURISTS **SANDBOARD DOWN GIANT DUNES** ON MANY OF **AFRICA'S BEACHES** AND **DESERTS.**

Surf's Up!

Before the luau that night, we decide to take a surfing lesson to build up our appetite. Our teacher,

"_____ Bill," teaches us a(n) _____ trick called hang _____ .
    ocean animal   *adjective*   *number*

I'm scared at first, but then I see this _____ wave coming at me. I jump on to my board,
                                                                   adjective

face _____ , put my _____ at the front edge of the board, and
      direction   *body part, plural*

_____ that wave like a pro. I feel like I'm the _____ of _____ !
    verb   *royal title*   *country name*

Then I hear _____ shout, "Check it out!" (S)he _____ over a pair of
            friend's name   *verb ending in –s*

_____ _____ in the water and is suddenly surfing on my board with me.
    animal, plural   *verb ending in –ing*

Holding _____ , we both look over to our right. _____ Bill is
       body part, plural   *same ocean animal*

using just one _____ to balance on his board. Dude, _____
             animal body part   *adjective ending in –est*

surfing lesson *ever.*

17

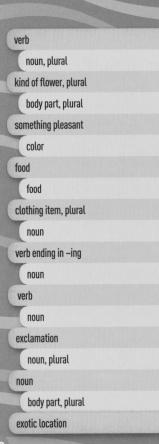

- verb
  - noun, plural
- kind of flower, plural
  - body part, plural
- something pleasant
  - color
- food
  - food
- clothing item, plural
  - noun
- verb ending in –ing
  - noun
- verb
  - noun
- exclamation
  - noun, plural
- noun
  - body part, plural
- exotic location

Fun Fact! A LAW ONCE MADE IT **ILLEGAL** TO SING LOUDLY OUTSIDE AFTER SUNSET IN HAWAII.

Let's Luau

Surfing was fun, but now it's time to _____ at the luau. When we arrive, _____ made of
_____(verb)_____   _____(noun, plural)_____

_____ are placed around our _____ . They smell like _____ .
(kind of flower, plural)   (body part, plural)   (something pleasant)

A buffet of traditional luau foods is nearby—I see bowls of grilled _____ _____ and
                                                                    (color)   (food)

_____ on buns, plus something that looks like chicken. Women in _____ made
(food)   (clothing item, plural)

of _____ are _____ as the _____ sets in the sky. Next, some dancers
   (noun)   (verb ending in –ing)   (noun)

_____ sticks lit with _____ into the air. "_____ !" we cry. We must
(verb)   (noun)   (exclamation)

have been too loud, though. A grumpy old man arrives, yelling, "Lower your _____ ! Some
                                                                            (noun, plural)

people are trying to sleep." Before he can storm off, we offer to teach him how to do the _____
                                                                                          (noun)

dance as an apology. He looks skeptical, but soon he's shaking his _____ and having a blast!
                                                                    (body part, plural)

What a great way to end our trip in _____ .
                                    (exotic location)

- friend's name
- adjective
- noun
- noun
- color
- adjective
- noun
- land animal
- animal, plural
- adjective
- size
- adjective
- verb ending in –ing
- body part, plural
- large animal
- verb
- adjective

Fun Fact!

THE **INGREDIENT** THAT MAKES MOST PEANUT BUTTER **SPREADABLE** COMES FROM **SEAWEED.**

_____ and I are back underwater in our trusty submarine. Suddenly, it starts to get
              friend's name

_____ inside our vehicle. We look through the _____ and see a forest—a kelp forest!
   adjective   noun

The _____-like kelp is _____ and _____. We feel like we're in an
        noun   color   adjective

underwater _____. I almost expect to see a(n) _____. We swim into the water
              noun   land animal

for a closer look. There are all kinds of cool marine life among the seaweed, like playful _____,
                                                                                              animal, plural

_____ sea dragons, _____ king crabs, and some _____-looking soft-bodied
     adjective   size   adjective

nudibranchs. We're _____ at the _____ on a king crab when we spot
                    verb ending in –ing   body part, plural

a(n) _____ pod nearby. Some of them even _____ at me! As cool as the kelp forest
        large animal   verb

is, a(n) _____-shaped object deep below gets our attention—we swim off to find out what it is.
            adjective

name of body of water

noun

adjective

noun

piece of furniture, plural

noun

verb

color

noun, plural

famous person

verb

verb ending in –ing

funny noise

animal

adverb ending in –ly

body part, plural

verb

Fun Fact! THE **WORLD'S OCEANS** CONTAIN ENOUGH GOLD TO GIVE **TWO POUNDS** (900 G) TO **EVERY PERSON** ON THE PLANET.

You wouldn't believe what we found at the bottom of the _____ . A shipwreck!

name of body of water

And not just any shipwreck—a famous one. We swim through the _____ to see what we can find.

noun

My favorite part is an old ballroom with a(n) _____-looking _____ , lots of old-fashioned

adjective / noun

_____ , and plenty of fish. Best of all, we find a large wooden _____ .

piece of furniture, plural / noun

We _____ to open it, but finally manage to lift off the top. Inside are lots and lots of _____

verb / color

_____—we're as rich as _____ ! Both of us grab a handful and

noun, plural / famous person

_____ our treasure. While we're _____ , we hear a _____ .

verb / verb ending in –ing / funny noise

A giant _____ has _____ wrapped its _____

animal / adverb ending in –ly / body part, plural

around the treasure! Uh-oh. We _____ out of there—and fast!

verb

animal

    noun

continent

    plant, plural

animal, plural

    verb ending in –ing

adjective

    bird

color

    body part, plural

fruit, plural

    type of transportation

past-tense verb

    noun, plural

clothing item

    verb ending in –ing

verb

    adverb ending in –ly

verb ending in –ing

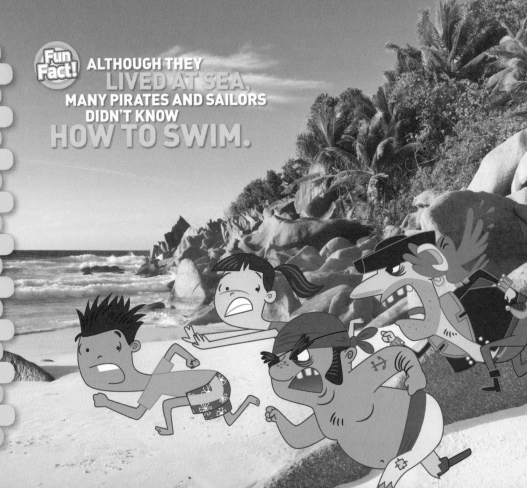

Fun Fact! ALTHOUGH THEY LIVED AT SEA, MANY PIRATES AND SAILORS DIDN'T KNOW HOW TO SWIM.

See you later, giant _____ ! We swim ashore, leaving the creepy creature behind. We find
　　　　　　　　　　　　　　　　animal

ourselves on a(n) _____ off the coast of _____— which is deserted, aside from lots of
　　　　　　　　　noun　　　　　　　　　　　　continent

_____ , _____ , and shells, of course. Then we hear _____ .
　plant, plural　　　　　　　animal, plural　　　　　　　　　　　　　　　　　　　　　verb ending in –ing

A group of _____-looking pirates is coming toward us! One of the pirates has a(n) _____
　　　　　　　adjective　　　　　　　　　　　　　　　　　　　　　　　　　　　　　　　　　　　bird

on its shoulder, one has a(n) _____ tooth, and several have peg-_____ and bad sunburns.
　　　　　　　　　　　　　　　color　　　　　　　　　　　　　　　　body part, plural

They are the color of bright _____! The pirates' _____ has _____ ,
　　　　　　　　　　　　　　fruit, plural　　　　　　　　　type of transportation　　　　past-tense verb

and they lost all of their _____. One of the pirates spots the treasure in my
　　　　　　　　　　　　noun, plural

_____ . The pirates start _____ us! We _____
　clothing item　　　　　　　　　　　　verb ending in –ing　　　　　　　　verb

our treasure at them and start _____ _____ back to our vehicle.
　　　　　　　　　　　　　　adverb ending in –ly　　　verb ending in –ing

I hope these pesky pirates can't swim!

verb ending in –ing

past-tense verb

noun

long distance

adjective

verb ending in –ing

size

scary animal

same animal

verb ending in –ing

noun

exclamation

feeling

verb

same animal

verb ending in –s

body part

adverb ending in –ly

body part, plural

Fun Fact! **SHARKS** **LIVED ON EARTH MORE THAN** **170 MILLION YEARS** **BEFORE DINOSAURS.**

Tangled!

We are safely back in our vehicle. It's _____ (verb ending in –ing) along, when suddenly it gets _____ (past-tense verb)

in something—a big, knotted _____ (noun) . We don't know what to do. There's no one around for

_____ (long distance) . To make things worse, a(n) _____ (adjective) -looking shape with _____ (verb ending in –ing)

eyes and _____ (size) teeth is moving closer to us. It's a(n) _____ (scary animal) ! The _____ (same animal)

starts _____ (verb ending in –ing) on the _____ (noun) covering our vehicle. "_____ (exclamation) !" we yell,

holding each other in _____ (feeling) . But all the animal does is make a hole big enough for our vehicle

to _____ (verb) through. The _____ (same animal) _____ (verb ending in –s) at us and wiggles its

_____ (body part) before swimming _____ (adverb ending in –ly) away. Guess this creature is nicer than it looks.

Never judge an animal by the size of its _____ (body part, plural) .

- large number
  - adjective
- verb ending in –ing
  - something cold, plural
- animal, plural
  - verb
- animal, plural
  - verb ending in –ed
- verb ending in –ing
  - temperature
- exclamation
  - clothing item, plural
- color
  - clothing item, plural
- body part, plural
  - verb
- liquid
  - silly word

Fun Fact! SOME PENGUINS CAN DIVE 1,000 FEET (305 M) DEEP— THAT'S ABOUT 150 TIMES DEEPER THAN AN OLYMPIC SWIMMING POOL.

What feels like _____ days passes without us seeing anyone or anything. But then weird,
                  large number

_____ shapes start blocking our vehicle's underwater path. Where are we? _____
 adjective   verb ending in –ing

to the surface, we see _____ and snow everywhere. We're in Antarctica! A group of
                        something cold, plural

loud _____ lounge on a nearby piece of ice. We pass them and _____ on the snowy
      animal, plural   verb

shore and look around. A group of black-and-white _____ have _____ around a
                                                    animal, plural   verb ending in –ed

cliff not far from us. Some of the animals begin _____ into the _____ water.
                                                  verb ending in –ing   temperature

"_____!" they yell at us. We hurry to join them—good thing we have _____
   exclamation   clothing item, plural

on under our scuba gear. We layer on _____ _____ and scarves too.
                                       color   clothing item, plural

Holding _____, we _____ into the icy _____ and shout
         body part, plural   verb   liquid

"_____!" Brrr!
   silly word

- friend's name
- verb ending in –ing
- body of water
- temperature
- liquid
- verb ending in –ing
- funny noise
- adjective
- verb ending in –ing
- size
- noun, plural
- verb
- verb
- noun
- verb
- body part, plural
- cold place

Fun Fact!

THE AIR TRAPPED INSIDE AN ICEBERG CAN BE THOUSANDS OF YEARS OLD.

The Great Penguin Rescue

Talk about a cool experience—literally. _____ and I are _____ in the
_____(friend's name)_____ _____(verb ending in –ing)_____

chilly waters of the _____ with a bunch of penguins. They don't seem to mind
_____(body of water)_____

the _____ _____ , but we sure do. We can't stop _____ .
(temperature) _(liquid)_ _____(verb ending in –ing)_____

We're about to get out, but then we hear a(n) _____ coming from far away.
_____(funny noise)_____

A(n) _____ baby penguin is _____ on a(n) _____ piece of a glacier! It's drifting
(adjective) _____(verb ending in –ing)_____ _(size)_

farther away from its _____ and the shore. We quickly _____ back to our boat.
_____(noun, plural)_____ _(verb)_

We _____ the boat behind the glacier piece to push it—and the baby—back toward the
(verb)

shore. When the baby gets closer to the _____ , it hops off and reunites with its family.
(noun)

We _____ our _____ , happy to see them together again.
(verb) _____(body part, plural)_____

_____ is great, but it's too cold—on to warmer waters!
(cold place)

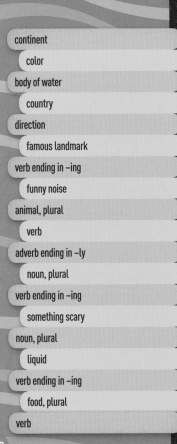

continent

color

body of water

country

direction

famous landmark

verb ending in –ing

funny noise

animal, plural

verb

adverb ending in –ly

noun, plural

verb ending in –ing

something scary

noun, plural

liquid

verb ending in –ing

food, plural

verb

Fun Fact! **BIZARRE CREATURES,** SUCH AS **CLAMS** AS BIG AS **DINNER PLATES,** LIVE NEAR **HYDROTHERMAL** VENTS.

Underwater Blast

We leave _____ (continent) and all of its ice behind. Soon, we're in the warm _____ (color)

_____ (body of water). We think we're close to _____ (country), so we point our vehicle _____ (direction) to

get there. We both want to see _____ (famous landmark). Suddenly, we feel some _____ (verb ending in –ing)

and hear a low _____ (funny noise). Several schools of _____ (animal, plural) swim quickly by us, headed in

the opposite direction. We _____ (verb) out of the submarine to look for the source of the sounds. The noise

gets louder, so we stop and look _____ (adverb ending in –ly) ahead of us. A giant cloud of _____ (noun, plural) is

_____ (verb ending in –ing) toward us. Is it a(n) _____ (something scary) monster? Then the cloud fades away.

In the distance, we see several _____ (noun, plural) on the ocean floor, with _____ (liquid) _____ (verb ending in –ing)

out of them—they're hydrothermal vents. We get out some _____ (food, plural) and

_____ (verb) them over the hot vents. Yum!

- verb ending in –s
  - famous landmark
- noun, plural
  - noun, plural
- number
  - past-tense verb
- silly word
  - famous city
- teacher's name
  - favorite subject
- large number
  - past-tense verb
- body of water
  - friend's name
- adjective ending in –est
  - animal, plural
- animal, plural

ACCORDING TO LEGEND, THE **LOST CITY OF ATLANTIS** HAD PEOPLE WHO WERE **HALF-GOD** AND **HALF-HUMAN.**

FOR RENT

WELCOME TO **ATLANTIS** "THE CITY ~~IN~~ UNDER THE SEA"

SPEED LIMIT XXV

NO CHARIOT PARKING IX TIL V TUESDAY

The Lost City

Having an underwater barbecue is crazy enough. But when the smoke _____ (verb ending in –s),

we see something even crazier—buildings at the bottom of the ocean! There is practically a whole city

before us. The buildings remind me of _____ (famous landmark). Besides buildings, there are what

looks like _____ (noun, plural) and _____ (noun, plural). We can make out _____ (number) letter(s)

_____ (past-tense verb) into one of the buildings. The sign reads: "_____ (silly word)." These are

the first letters of _____ (famous city), which we learned about in _____ (teacher's name)'s

_____ (favorite subject) class. It supposedly existed _____ (large number) years ago, before it _____ (past-tense verb)

into the _____ (body of water). Could it be? Did _____ (friend's name) and I solve one of history's

_____ (adjective ending in –est) mysteries? The _____ (animal, plural) and _____ (animal, plural)

swimming nearby aren't talking.

35

famous city

country

adjective

silly word

noun

verb ending in –ing

same silly word

verb

noun, plural

body part, plural

noun, plural

adjective

temperature

verb

color

noun, plural

noun

celebrity's name

small sea creature

Fun Fact! IN DEEP **UNDERWATER CAVES,** TIDES CAN WHIP UP **WHIRLPOOLS** THAT LOOK LIKE WATER SWIRLING DOWN GIANT BATHTUB DRAINS.

Crystal Cave

We leave underwater _____ behind and head for _____ .
                       famous city   *country*

We've heard _____ stories about _____ Cave, the largest _____ .
            adjective   *silly word*   *noun*

cave in the world. We want to try cave-_____ . _____ Cave is dark and hard
                                    verb ending in –ing   *same silly word*

to _____ in, though. Good thing we're prepared—we both are wearing _____
   verb   *noun, plural*

on our _____ that have _____ strapped to them. We climb down the
       body part, plural   *noun, plural*

_____ entrance of the cave, into the _____ waters. Then we begin to _____ .
adjective   *temperature*   *verb*

We stare in amazement at the bright _____ _____ as we sink deeper and make
                                    color   *noun, plural*

turn after turn. Soon, we're lost. What if we can't find our way back? We've heard rumors that this cave is

haunted by a(n) _____ that looks like _____ . Luckily, a friendly
                noun   *celebrity's name*

_____ named Sandy helps us find our way out. We've never been happier to be above water!
small sea creature

liquid

noun

noun

body part

silly word

adjective

verb ending in –ing

verb ending in –ing

adjective

verb

animal body part

noun, plural

small sea creature, plural

body part, plural

verb ending in –s

body part

Fun Fact! DOLPHINS CAN HEAR SOUNDS UNDERWATER THAT ARE 15 MILES (24 KM) AWAY.

It's nice to be above _____ for a bit. We're relaxing in the _____ .
                        liquid   noun

I'm slathering _____ on my _____ when I hear a _____ and look
                 noun   body part   silly word

overboard to see a(n) _____ group of dolphins _____ near us.
                        adjective   verb ending in –ing

Despite all the things we've done on our trip, we still haven't swam with dolphins! Now is our chance.

_____ overboard, we're surrounded by the _____ animals. We both _____
verb ending in –ing   adjective   verb

a(n) _____ with each hand, and off we go! Some of the other dolphins show off for us by doing
       animal body part

awesome _____ and balancing _____ on their _____ .
          noun, plural   small sea creature, plural   body part, plural

One of them even _____ my _____ .
                   verb ending in –s   body part

Forget puppy love. I've got a case of dolphin love.

famous athlete

friend's name

verb

noun

continent

same verb

verb ending in –ing

insect

color

scary animal

past-tense verb

noun

something gross

color

clothing item

exclamation

past-tense verb

animal

same famous athlete

Fun Fact! AUSTRALIA'S GREAT BARRIER REEF CAN BE SEEN FROM SPACE.

Hide-and-Reef-Seek

No ocean adventure is complete without a trip to the _____ Reef, the world's largest coral
famous athlete

reef system. _____ suggests we play "I _____." There's no better place to play than among
friend's name _verb_

the _____ off the coast of _____ . "I _____," I say, pointing out
noun _continent_ _same verb_

supercool animals _____ near us—my favorite is the _____ fish. My friend
verb ending in –ing _insect_

guesses them all except the _____-tipped _____ that _____ away.
color _scary animal_ _past-tense verb_

Next, we play "Hide-and-Seek." I look behind the _____ and inside the school of _____
noun _something gross_

fish, but I can't find my friend anywhere. Then I see something _____ flash by. Thinking it's my
color

friend's _____ , I shout, " _____ !" I'm _____ to see
clothing item _exclamation_ _past-tense verb_

a(n) _____ instead—one of the most venomous animals in the world. Now seems
animal

like a good time to say goodbye to _____ Reef!
same famous athlete

- verb
  - favorite food
- adjective
  - foreign language
- country
  - verb ending in –ing
- noun
  - noun
- verb ending in –ing
  - animal
- exclamation
  - same favorite food, plural
- verb
  - color
- bird
  - verb ending in –ing
- famous singer
  - adjective
- body part, plural

Fun Fact! SCUBA DIVERS CAN **SEND POSTCARDS** FROM A MAILBOX OFF THE **COAST OF JAPAN** THAT'S NEARLY **33 FEET** (10 M) UNDERWATER.

Snack Attack

We realize that we haven't had anything to eat since Mermaid-ville. We spot land, so we pull ashore to

_____ for _____ . There is a(n) _____ -looking lighthouse that seems very
    verb   favorite food   adjective

_____ . We must be in _____ . We take a tour of the lighthouse, _____
  foreign language   country   verb ending in –ing

the _____ at the top. Then we go to the _____ . My stomach is _____ like
    noun   noun   verb ending in –ing

a(n) _____ . "_____ !" I shout. A café has _____ . We _____ outside
    animal   exclamation   same favorite food, plural   verb

with our food, but before I can take a bite, a(n) _____ -tailed _____ swoops in from above and
                                 color   bird

whisks away the snack. Another bird swoops in for my friend's food. We duck, _____ the
                                              verb ending in –ing

bird away, but it's too late. Both snacks are gone. My stomach now sounds like _____ 's last
                                            famous singer

concert. We go back inside for more food, and this time, we stay inside. The _____ birds are
                                            adjective

waiting outside with scary expressions on their _____ .
                                    body part, plural

- name of body of water
- verb ending in –s
- adverb ending in –ly
- exclamation
- famous landmark
- body part, plural
- noun
- adjective
- animal
- verb
- silly word
- same body of water
- past-tense verb
- color
- noun, plural
- small sea creature, plural
- noun, plural
- plant, plural

Fun Fact! A **JELLYFISH** CAN BE AS SMALL AS A **THIMBLE** OR AS LARGE AS **TWO** WASHING MACHINES.

The Oceanic Express

After finally eating, we're back underwater again. We want to cross the _____ , but our
name of body of water

submarine is making some strange sounds. It _____ forward so _____
verb ending in –s   adverb ending in –ly

that we yell, "_____ !" Then we drop from what seems like the height of the
exclamation

_____ . Feeling sick to our _____ , we decide to take the sub to a(n)
famous landmark   body part, plural

_____ -repair shop. A(n) _____ jellyfish and a friendly _____ get the vehicle fixed fast.
noun   adjective   animal

The jellyfish suggests we _____ onboard the _____ train for a quick trip
verb   silly word

across the _____ —our vehicle will be _____ safely in the back, and
same body of water   past-tense verb

we'll be able to meet lots of awesome ocean animals like _____ gobies, sea _____ ,
color   noun, plural

and colorful _____ . Best of all, the seats are made of _____ and are
small sea creature, plural   noun, plural

built above floating _____ . We're on our way!
plant, plural

- verb
  - hometown
- friend's name
  - adjective
- animal, plural
  - past-tense verb
- animal
  - pet
- silly name
  - liquid
- noun
  - same noun
- verb
  - verb ending in –ing
- body part, plural
  - noun, plural
- favorite song

Fun Fact! RESEARCHERS ESTIMATE THAT AROUND **4,000 SPECIES** OF OCEAN FISH HAVE YET TO BE **DISCOVERED.**

Beach-Bound

Feeling homesick—or is it seasick?—we _____ it's time we go back to _____ .
_____(verb)_____   _____(hometown)_____

_____ and I have been on a(n) _____ adventure through the ocean. We swam
___(friend's name)___   ___(adjective)___

with _____ , _____ from pirates, saw an underwater eruption, and even rescued
___(animal, plural)___   ___(past-tense verb)___

a baby _____ . But I miss my _____ , _____ , and the taste of _____
_____(animal)_____   ____(pet)____   ___(silly name)___   ___(liquid)___

without salt. Unsure of what to do to get home, we search the vehicle. Near the "PRESS ME" _____ ,
                                                                                    ___(noun)___

we find another _____ that says, "HOME." We _____ it. The submarine quickly rises out
____(same noun)____   ___(verb)___

of the water and turns into a boat again. _____ our _____ from the sun, we
                              ___(verb ending in –ing)___   ___(body part, plural)___

look around to see where we are. In the distance, we spot my parents, still asleep in their

_____ . How long have they been sleeping? Humming
___(noun, plural)___

"_____ ," we dive in together for one last swim.
___(favorite song)___

How to Play Funny Fill-In!

Love to create amazing stories? Good, because this one stars YOU. Get ready to laugh with all your friends—you can play with as many people as you want! Make sure to keep this book on your shelf. You'll want to read it again and again!

Are You Ready to Laugh?

- One person picks a story—you can start at the beginning, the middle, or the end of the book.

- Ask a friend to call out a word that the space asks for—noun, verb, or something else—and write it in the blank space. If there's more than one person, ask the next person to say a word. Extra points for creativity!

- When all the spaces are filled in, you have your very own Funny Fill-In. Read it out loud for a laugh.

- Want to play by yourself? Just fold over the page and use the cardboard insert at the back as a writing pad. Fill in the blank parts of speech list, and copy your answers into the story.

Fun Fact! Make sure you check out the amazing **Fun Facts** that appear on every page!

To play the game, you'll need to know how to form sentences. This list of the parts of speech and the examples will help you get started:

Noun: The name of a person, place, thing, or idea
Examples: tree, mouth, creature
*The **ocean** is full of colorful **fish**.*

Adjective: A word that describes a noun or pronoun
Examples: green, lazy, friendly
*My **silly** dog won't stop laughing!*

Verb: An action word. In the present tense, a verb usually ends in –s or –ing. If the space asks for past tense, changing the vowel or adding a –d or –ed to the end usually will set the sentence in the past.
Examples: swim, hide, play (present tense);
biked, rode, jumped (past tense)
*The giraffe **skips** across the savanna.*
*The flower **opened** after the rain.*

Adverb: A word that describes a verb and usually ends in –ly
Examples: quickly, lazily, soundlessly
*Kelley **greedily** ate all the carrots.*

Plural: More than one
Examples: mice, telephones, wrenches
*Why are all the **doors** closing?*

Silly Word or Exclamation: A funny sound, a made-up word, a word you think is totally weird, or a noise someone or something might make
Examples: Ouch! No way! Foozleduzzle! Yikes!
*"**Darn!**" shouted Jim. "These cupcakes are sour!"*

Specific Words: There are many more ways to make your story hilarious. When asked for something like a number, animal, or body part, write in something you think is especially funny.

adjective

    animal

verb ending in –ing

    verb

friend's name

    relative's name

number

    adjective

silly word

    verb

direction

    one of the Wonders of the World

body part

    your name

celebrity's name

    kind of lunch meat

favorite movie

    favorite snack

Fun Fact! MORE THAN **60,000** PEOPLE ARE **FLYING OVER** THE UNITED STATES IN AIRPLANES **RIGHT NOW.**

No way! I won the _____ _____ contest! I can't believe it. For my prize, I'll be _____
adjective   *animal*   *verb ending in –ing*

around the world to _____ all the coolest animals. Of course, I'm bringing _____ .
verb   *friend's name*

Unfortunately, there's so much luggage, it takes _____ and _____ neighbors to jam it
relative's name   *number*

all into the car. Finally on the road, everything is going as planned. Until the GPS goes _____ and
adjective

starts saying things like, "_____ _____ _____." Following the bewildering
silly word   *verb*   *direction*

commands, we pass _____ ! But, finally, the airport comes into view. Just as I
one of the Wonders of the World

squeeze my _____ into the airplane seat, the loudspeaker crackles and I hear, "_____ ,
body part   *your name*

raise your hand." Turns out, _____ has decided (s)he only rides on airplanes the color of
celebrity's name

_____ . We get moved to his/her first class seats! Seat back, feet up, _____
kind of lunch meat   *favorite movie*

on the screen, munching on _____ —I could get used to this!
favorite snack

- verb ending in –ing
  - friend's name
- favorite song
  - animal
- noun
  - famous sports player
- verb
  - body part
- loud noise
  - color
- adjective
  - number
- noun
  - something smelly
- item of clothing, plural
  - adjective
- adjective
  - verb ending in –ing
- singer's name

 Fun Fact!

WHEN A BROWN BEAR STANDS ON ITS HIND LEGS, IT'S NOT ALWAYS TRYING TO BE THREATENING. IT'S OFTEN JUST GETTING A BETTER LOOK AT ITS SURROUNDINGS.

Over-BEAR-ing Family Photo

Our first stop, backpacking in Alaska! With my camera _____ (verb ending in –ing) around my neck, _____ (friend's name) is singing _____ (favorite song) as we walk down the trail. Too bad that his/her singing sounds more like a _____ (animal). I decide to check out a cool _____ (noun) I see in the distance. But, as I walk farther, a bear bigger than _____ (famous sports player) _____ (verb) in front of me. I am so scared, I feel as if my _____ (body part) is jelly! Suddenly, I hear a(n) _____ (loud noise), and _____ (color) fur and _____ (adjective) teeth surround me. _____ (number) bears are so close I can feel their _____ (noun) and smell their _____ (something smelly) breath! Then the bears put on wacky _____ (item of clothing, plural) and _____ (adjective) sunglasses. They start posing with _____ (adjective) smiles as if they're on vacation! Finally, I realize they are _____ (verb ending in –ing) and want photos. Just then, my friend arrives, still singing. The bears join in. Mother Bear sounds just like _____ (singer's name)!

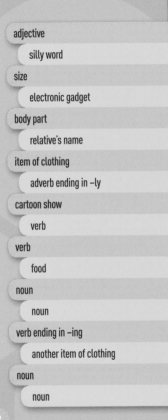

- adjective
  - silly word
- size
  - electronic gadget
- body part
  - relative's name
- item of clothing
  - adverb ending in –ly
- cartoon show
  - verb
- verb
  - food
- noun
  - noun
- verb ending in –ing
  - another item of clothing
- noun
  - noun

Fun Fact! BLACK-TAILED PRAIRIE DOGS **WARN EACH OTHER** AT THE **FIRST SIGN** OF **PREDATORS,** SUCH AS A HUNGRY HAWK OR BLACK-FOOTED FERRET.

Prairie Dog Pranksters

The North American grasslands are _____ . Thanks to prankster prairie dogs, I now have a new video.
<u>adjective</u>

Just not exactly what I'd hoped. As we crept into _____ -ville, a(n) _____ prairie dog popped out
<u>silly word</u> <u>size</u>

of its burrow and snatched my _____ . When I dove into the praire dog's tunnel, my
<u>electronic gadget</u>

_____ got wedged in the opening. _____ grabbed my feet but instead accidentally
<u>body part</u> <u>relative's name</u>

pulled off my _____ . The prairie dog took a picture, then _____ disappeared
<u>item of clothing</u> <u>adverb ending in –ly</u>

underground. What happened next was like a _____ chase. I'd _____ . The animal
<u>cartoon show</u> <u>verb</u>

would _____ . Each time, its friend snapped pictures. They grabbed my _____ , my
<u>verb</u> <u>food</u>

_____ , and my favorite _____ ! Finally, a prairie dog stood on top of me, _____
<u>noun</u> <u>noun</u> <u>verb ending in –ing</u>

my cellphone, recording video, and wearing my _____ , my _____ , and even my
<u>another item of clothing</u> <u>noun</u>

_____ . Suddenly, it started typing on my phone. It hit "Send." Wouldn't you know, the video went viral!
<u>noun</u>

small number

    pop star

loud noise

    noun

friend's name

    noun

piece of furniture

    verb ending in –ing

adjective

    body part

liquid

    verb ending in –ing

verb

    adjective

something gross

    animal, plural

verb

    animal

 Fun Fact! A DAIRY COW **PRODUCES** ABOUT **100,000 GLASSES OF MILK** IN ITS LIFETIME.

Farm Frenzy

At _____ a.m., we pile into the car for a canoe trip. We are singing along to _____
small number   *pop star*

when we hear a(n) _____ . Our car has a flat _____ ! Soon, a pickup truck pulls
loud noise   *noun*

over. "I'm Farmer _____ . Can I offer y'all a ride?" the driver asks. That's how we spent
friend's name

the day on a _____ farm. I sit on a(n) _____ next to the farmer to learn to
noun   *piece of furniture*

milk a cow. But the cow starts _____ my hair. So instead, I try to run the _____
verb ending in –ing   *adjective*

milk machine. As I pull a lever, my _____ disconnects a tube, and _____
body part   *liquid*

starts _____ everywhere. I _____ from the machine, right into
verb ending in –ing   *verb*

a(n) _____ pile of _____ . A bunch of _____
adjective   *something gross*   *animal, plural*

run to lap up the spill, so I _____ toward the door. On the way,
verb

I slip and fall into the _____ pen. Who knew a farm was this wild?
animal

- something scary
  - friend's name
- noun
  - relative's name
- adverb ending in –ly
  - sound
- verb
  - something gross
- same friend
  - something silly
- verb
  - sports star
- adverb ending in –ly
  - feeling
- number
  - toy
- adjective

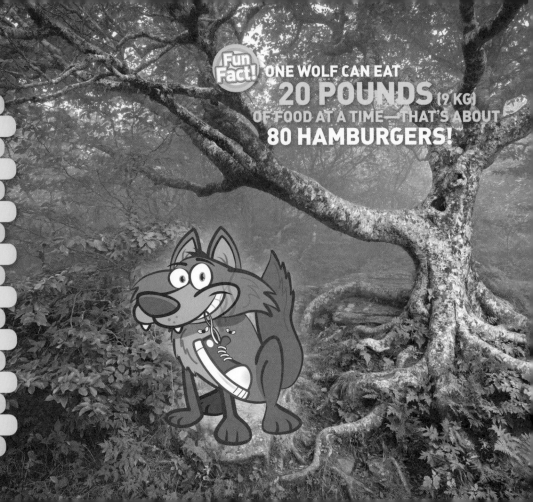

Fun Fact! ONE WOLF CAN EAT **20 POUNDS** (9 KG) OF FOOD AT A TIME—THAT'S ABOUT **80 HAMBURGERS!**

Wolf Games

Towering over us, the shaggy wolf casts a shadow creepier than _____ . _____
                                                               something scary   friend's name

immediately climbs up a(n) _____ , and I manage to grab on to a tree limb. While I dangle like
                                                 noun

_____ 's ugly earrings, the wolf snaps at my feet. Panicking, I _____
                  relative's name   adverb ending in –ly

fling my shoe. The creature catches it with a loud _____ and _____ it. Dropping to
                                             sound   verb

the ground, I run, but choke on the overpowering smell of _____ odor from the shoe.
                                                      something gross

_____ yells, "_____," and _____ his/her shoe.
            same friend   something silly   verb

The wolf catches it in midair like _____! _____ carrying
                                      sports star   adverb ending in –ly

the shoe, the wolf is as _____ as a _____-year-old with a new _____ .
                        feeling   number   toy

A game of fetch is what this pooch wants! Our shoes end up a bit _____ , but we have fun
                                                           adjective

playing with our new friend.

AN ALLIGATOR **GROWS** ABOUT 3,000 TEETH IN A LIFETIME.

- adjective
  - noun, plural
- adjective
  - verb
- noun
  - body part
- animal
  - number
- ice-cream flavor
  - verb
- friend's name
  - something gross
- mythical creature
  - liquid
- noun
  - adverb ending in –ly
- verb
  - same friend

Dangerous Dentistry

My next adventure is in the swampy Florida Everglades! Our boat skims across the _____ water.
(adjective)

Mosquitoes as big as _____ zoom by our heads. Suddenly, a(n) _____ alligator pops
(noun, plural)   (adjective)

out of the water! I think he is going to _____ me. Instead, he sobs like a(n) _____ and
(verb)   (noun)

points to his mouth with his _____. Fortunately, I've seen every episode of _____
(body part)   (animal)

Whisperer on channel _____, so I know his tooth hurts. But when I get close with my _____-
(number)   (ice-cream flavor)

flavored dental floss, he _____ his mouth shut. Just then, _____ slips
(verb)   (friend's name)

on _____, shrieks like a _____, then falls into some _____.
(something gross)   (mythical creature)   (liquid)

The alligator laughs so hard his mouth opens wider than a(n) _____. Here's my chance!
(noun)

I _____ lasso the tooth. It pops right out. Just then, the alligator's mom _____
(adverb ending in –ly)   (verb)

through the water toward _____. That's how I discover my friend is faster than a boat!
(same friend)

15

your weight

large number

friend's name

adjective

color

color

adjective

feeling

sound ending in –ing

adverb ending in –ly

number

direction

adjective

favorite frozen dessert

verb

famous artist

Fun Fact! POLAR BEARS HAVE **TRANSPARENT HAIR** WITH A HOLLOW CORE THAT **REFLECTS SUNLIGHT,** MAKING THEM APPEAR TO BE WHITE; THEIR SKIN IS **ACTUALLY BLACK!**

Polar Art Attack

Next stop, the Arctic Circle! Dragging _____ of paint behind me, I ask, "Why bring _____

your weight · large number

colors to paint a snowy Arctic landscape?" Instead of answering, _____

friend's name

hurls _____ snowballs at me. This is my chance to add some color, I think. So I throw

adjective

half-frozen globs of _____ and _____ paint at my friend. One is a direct hit. The other

color · color

misses, and a young polar bear now coated in _____ paint looks _____ .

adjective · feeling

_____ , the bear snatches an armful of paint. It _____ throws _____

sound ending in –ing · adverb ending in –ly · number

paintballs _____ , hitting another _____ bear. The glare of the second

direction · adjective

startled and splattered bear is colder than _____ . We relax when its laugh

favorite frozen dessert

_____ through the air. Then it starts the world's best paintball fight—ever.

verb

By the time we ran out of paint, we'd created _____ polar bears!

famous artist

- animal sound
  - friend's name
- adjective ending in –est
  - noun
- something soft
  - mythical creature, plural
- baby animal, plural
  - kind of candy
- pet's name
  - silly word
- verb
  - verb
- something scary
  - animal, plural
- something sharp
  - adjective
- verb
  - noun

Fun Fact!

EUROPE IS THE SECOND SMALLEST CONTINENT— BUT ITS COASTLINE OF SOME 24,000 MILES (38,000 KM) WOULD NEARLY STRETCH AROUND THE EARTH.

Cute Overload

We're trekking across the European countryside, and as we round the hedge, a soft _____ ,
                                                                                    animal sound

fills the air. _____ and I creep toward the sweet sound. Hanging out along a river are the world's
              friend's name

_____ creatures. Their _____ and soft _____ invite us
adjective ending in –est   *noun*   *something soft*

closer. Some wrestle like _____ . Others cuddle like _____ .
                          mythical creature, plural   *baby animal, plural*

And, they smell like _____ . One reminds me of _____ . I can't help it,
                     kind of candy   *pet's name*

I yell, "_____ !" All eyes _____ at us. That's when those sweet
        silly word   *verb*

fuzzy faces _____ into _____ ! Now, a herd of ferocious
            verb   *something scary*

stuffed _____ with _____ teeth and _____
        animal, plural   *something sharp*   *adjective*

claws are chasing us! We sprint and see the edge of a cliff—we _____ , splashing
                                                               verb

into the water below. Never judge a _____ by its cute looks!
                                    noun

19

- type of transportation
  - relative's name
- loud noise
  - sharp object
- friend's name
  - three letters
- number
  - color
- verb
  - adjective ending in –est
- item of clothing, plural
  - electronic gadget, plural
- amount of time
  - number
- adverb ending in –ly
  - verb
- same three letters
  - noun, plural

 ADULT MALE MANDRILL MONKEYS HAVE RED-AND-BLUE NOSES. THE COLOR BECOMES BRIGHTER WHEN THEY ARE EXCITED OR UPSET.

Fun Fact!

Monkey Mechanics

It's our first day in Africa, and our safari _____ , which is older than _____ ,
                                          type of transportation   _relative's name_

rattles down the jungle road. Suddenly, all four tires pop with a(n) " _____ !" when we cross
                                                                       loud noise

_____ Point. _____ radios _____ -Primate tire service, which
sharp object   _friend's name_   _three letters_

advertises its mechanics are "terribly fast." Within seconds, I hear something. _____ _____
                                                                                 number   _color_

monkeys _____ from the trees. The _____ yanks us out of the vehicle.
         verb   _adjective ending in –est_

_____ and _____ fly through the air. Within
item of clothing, plural   _electronic gadget, plural_

_____ , a monkey hands me a $ _____ bill for the "terribly fast" service.
amount of time   _number_

The monkeys _____ _____ up the trees. True to its advertising,
             adverb ending in –ly   _verb_

_____ -Primate service is definitely fast. Unfortunately, it's really terrible, too.
same three letters

The monkeys replaced the flat tires with _____ !
                                          noun, plural

adjective

    celebrity's name

verb ending in –ing

    verb

number

    something silly

adverb ending in –ly

    verb

insect, plural

    food

noun

    kind of candy

adjective

    something gross

body part, plural

Fun Fact! THE **LARGEST** LAND ANIMALS ON EARTH, AFRICAN ELEPHANTS USE THEIR **TRUNKS TO SPRAY WATER** TO KEEP COOL.

Elephant Edibles

Now that we've properly fixed our tires, I brought a ridiculously _____ bag of peanuts for our
adjective

drive over to the _____ Preserve to care for African elephants. But while everyone else
celebrity's name

is _____ , I decide to sneak a snack. I _____ into my first peanut when
verb ending in –ing   verb

_____ hungry elephants step out of the brush in front of the car. I shout, "_____"
number   something silly

and _____ drop the sack of snacks. Peanuts tumble everywhere. Elephant trunks
adverb ending in –ly

_____ all over me like _____ . But now the peanuts are gone, and the
verb   insect, plural

elephants are still hungry! Looking for more, the herd flips the jeep and shakes it like a box of _____
food

with a _____ inside. As I dangle from my seatbelt, _____ slip from my shirt
noun   kind of candy

pocket, to the elephants' delight. I now know they have _____ tongues and breath like
adjective

_____ . But they put me down safely and smack their _____ , leaving me starving!
something gross   body part, plural

23

liquid
_____

type of sandwich
_____

cool word
_____

movie star
_____

body part
_____

adjective
_____

adjective
_____

something gross
_____

fictional villain
_____

verb
_____

noun
_____

food
_____

silly word
_____

verb ending in –ing
_____

verb ending in –ing
_____

animal
_____

verb
_____

type of insect
_____

Fun Fact! AN **OSTRICH** CAN RUN AS FAST AS A **RACEHORSE.**

It's another hot African day, and I'm drinking lots of _____ . Nearby, I see a group of ostriches, and

liquid

I turn to see one munching on my _____ . "Wanna race?" he says. "_____ !"

type of sandwich
cool word

I say. My ostrich is _____ cool and so tall I only come up to his _____ .

movie star
body part

I'm tied to him with a _____ rope. The team next to us is _____ . There's a kid

adjective
adjective

who has _____ hair and a _____ -mean face. We _____

something gross
fictional villain
verb

down the track, when suddenly the tough kid sticks out a _____ , causing us to stumble into a

noun

_____ stand. The crowd chants, "_____ faces lose races!" _____ ,

food
silly word
verb ending in –ing

_____ , and sidestepping the mess, we cross the finish line, winning the race, and

verb ending in –ing

whiz to the next contest. We win the _____ dance contest, too! But I had better _____

animal
verb

the fine print for the _____ race I signed up for next!

type of insect

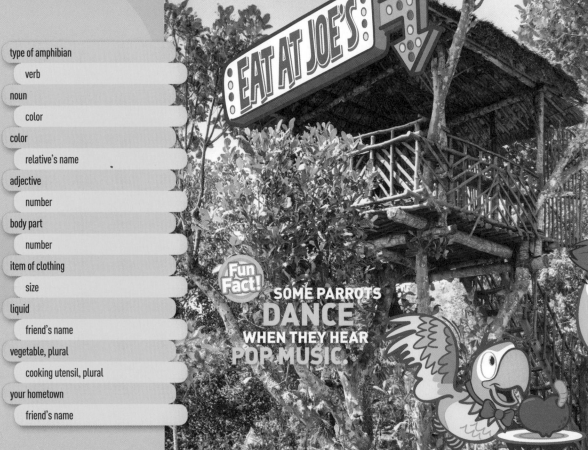

type of amphibian

    verb

noun

    color

color

    relative's name

adjective

    number

body part

    number

item of clothing

    size

liquid

    friend's name

vegetable, plural

    cooking utensil, plural

your hometown

    friend's name

Fun Fact! SOME PARROTS **DANCE** WHEN THEY HEAR POP MUSIC.

EAT AT JOE'S

Dropping In for **Dinner**

I've always wanted to see the South American rain forest! As I head to the _____ preserve,
                                                                          type of amphibian

I see there's an option to zip line there. I _____ faster than a _____ . Just then, a _____
                                            verb   noun   color

and _____ parrot lands on me and starts babbling faster than _____ about a feast.
    color   relative's name

All of a sudden, I notice other animals trying to hear what's on the _____ menu. There are
                                                                     adjective

_____ animals dangling from my _____ and _____ more latch
number   body part   number

on to my _____ . With so much weight, the zip line snaps! I drop into a _____ stewpot
         item of clothing   size

filled with _____ that smells like _____ 's feet! A crowd gathers. Some hold
            liquid   friend's name

_____ and sharp _____ . Someone says, "Ah, here is the exotic food from
vegetable, plural   cooking utensil, plural

_____ ." The crowd cheers. "Come, eat!" Uh-oh. Am I the exotic food? Just then, _____
your hometown   friend's name

walks up with the parrot. It says, "Come! Eat! My new friend, we set a special place for you!"

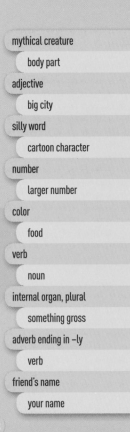

mythical creature
_____

body part
_____

adjective
_____

big city
_____

silly word
_____

cartoon character
_____

number
_____

larger number
_____

color
_____

food
_____

verb
_____

noun
_____

internal organ, plural
_____

something gross
_____

adverb ending in –ly
_____

verb
_____

friend's name
_____

your name
_____

Fun Fact! RAIN FORESTS ARE MOST "ALIVE" AT NIGHT— 80 PERCENT OF ALL THE ANIMAL ACTIVITY TAKES PLACE IN THE DARK.

The Coolest Species No One Ever Saw

Move over, _____ (mythical creature), you have competition! My hike through the remote South American

jungle has led me face-to-_____ (body part) with a brand-new species. Only, I'm sure no one will believe me.

It's the most _____ (adjective) creature I've ever seen. Its skin sparkles like _____ (big city) at night.

"_____ (silly word), is my name," it says in a _____ (cartoon character) -like voice. _____ (number) of its

_____ (larger number) arms glow _____ (color). Its legs remind me of a(n) _____ (food). All of its eyes

focus on me. Suddenly, it _____ (verb) through the air, whirling like a(n) _____ (noun),

and lands next to me. I could get over the eyes, arms, and visible _____ (internal organ, plural), but it smells

like _____ (something gross). "Want to know why I'm the coolest animal ever?" it _____ (adverb ending in –ly)

purrs. Before I can answer, my friends _____ (verb) through the trees, and it vanishes. No one believes

me, and _____ (friend's name) starts calling it the _____ (your name) -made-it-uppa monster!

noun

> friend's name

celebrity name, possessive

> fruit

adverb ending in –ly

> transportation, plural

verb

> noun

adjective

> something in nature, plural

verb

> body part

royal title

> sound, plural

adjective

> something you bring to the beach

favorite flavor

> adverb ending in –ly

Fun Fact! ANTS CAN LIFT AND CARRY MORE THAN 100 TIMES THEIR OWN WEIGHT.

Getting Away From It All

Temperatures are rising faster than a(n) _____ . _____ and I can't wait to get to
                                         noun   friend's name

_____ Paradise Beach, to relax and enjoy tropical _____ smoothies.
celebrity name, possessive   fruit

_____ pedaling through the jungle on _____ , we stop at an "Ant Crossing"
adverb ending in –ly   transportation, plural

sign. We _____ a line of ants carrying so much fruit it looks like a(n) _____ . Missing
           verb   noun

_____ beach time, I create a ramp from _____ . We _____
adjective   something in nature, plural   verb

over the ants and keep going. Then I see spots! A jaguar with an injured _____ blocks the path.
                                                                          body part

Fortunately, I'm _____ of the Wildcat First Aid Club, and I heal the injured animal.
                  royal title

When we're finally greeted by the beach's _____ , I need a(n) _____ drink.
                                            sound, plural   adjective

Just as I plop into my _____ , the ants march up with a _____
                       something you bring to the beach   favorite flavor

smoothie, and my new spotted friend _____ serves it. Now that's paradise!
                                      adverb ending in –ly

31

- sports player
  - sport
- adjective
  - size
- verb
  - adjective
- adjective
  - noun
- verb
  - liquid
- gymnastics move
  - flying animal
- relative's name
  - body part
- adverb ending in –ly
  - color
- same liquid
  - cool word

 Fun Fact! SOME **WILD DOLPHINS PLAY CATCH** WITH **COCONUTS.**

DUDE, Dolphin Surfing

I always knew I could surf like _____ , who plays _____ ! Showing off
                                      sports player   *sport*

my _____ moves, I didn't see the _____ dolphin until I _____ him.
        adjective   *size*   *verb*

"Dude," he said. "You've got some _____ moves, but I'm better!" Dolphins may rule the
                                        adjective

surf, but I am _____ . Catching the perfect _____ , I _____ through
                   adjective   *noun*   *verb*

the _____ like a pro. Next to me, the dolphin does a spectacular _____ .
        liquid   *gymnastics move*

Launching too high, I hit a _____ . Screeching like _____ , it grabs
                                flying animal   *relative's name*

on to me, covering my _____ . I nearly fall, but the animal flies away. I'm surfing faster than
                          body part

ever, but I _____ realize I'm not controlling my _____ board. That's
               adverb ending in -ly   *color*

because I'm surfing on the dolphin! Ripping through the _____ waves, we both rule the surf.
                                                            same liquid

This is _____ !
           cool word

33

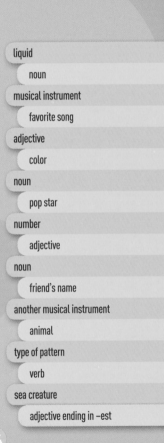

- liquid
  - noun
- musical instrument
  - favorite song
- adjective
  - color
- noun
  - pop star
- number
  - adjective
- noun
  - friend's name
- another musical instrument
  - animal
- type of pattern
  - verb
- sea creature
  - adjective ending in –est

Fun Fact! **CORAL REEFS** ARE CONSIDERED THE RAIN FORESTS OF THE SEA, BECAUSE THEY PROVIDE FOOD AND SHELTER FOR UP TO **25 PERCENT** OF ALL MARINE LIFE.

Rocking the Reef

The hum of the ocean takes on new meaning as I snorkel in _____ through an Indonesian coral
                                                            liquid

reef. Admiring coral more colorful than a(n) _____ , I swim around the nearest rock and hear a(n)
                                              noun

_____ -fish start playing _____ . Then I see a seahorse strumming sea grass like
musical instrument   favorite song

a(n) _____ guitar and a(n) _____ fish belting out a(n) _____ better than _____ .
     adjective   color   noun   pop star

The concert grows when _____ tube worms pop up as background singers. This band is just getting
                       number

started! Suddenly, an octopus appears in front of me and stretches across the coral to make a(n) _____
                                                                                                  adjective

drum so I can add a(n) _____ . _____ plays a snorkel like a(n) _____ , and
                      noun   friend's name   another musical instrument

a(n) _____ picks up the song's melody. A fiddler crab and electric eel rock the sea while
     animal

_____ fish _____ . I'm almost blown back when a(n) _____
type of pattern   verb   sea creature

hits the _____ final note! Download the ocean band's album . . . if you have "Sea"-Tunes!
         adjective ending in -est

number

    adjective

friend's name

    noun

liquid

    adjective

adjective ending in –er

    verb

something pointy

    same friend

something soft

    noun

verb ending in –ed

    something in nature

body part

    noise

noun

    adjective

Fun Fact! TIGERS CAN EAT **40 POUNDS** (18 KILOGRAMS) IN A SINGLE SITTING. AFTER A BIG MEAL, THEY CAN GO UP TO **ONE WEEK** WITHOUT EATING.

We're in India, and after our _____ -mile _____ hike, _____ and I are hotter than
                        (number)   (adjective)   (friend's name)

_____ . We get to the end and see a(n) _____ fountain guarded by—a tiger! "To quench your
  (noun)   (liquid)

thirst, you must answer first," announces the _____ tiger. "What gets _____ as it
                                              (adjective)   (adjective ending in -er)

_____ ?" the big cat asks through _____ teeth. _____
  (verb)   (something pointy)   (same friend)

croaks, "A _____ !" The tiger nods, and immediately asks, "What runs all the _____
           (something soft)   (noun)

and never gets _____ ?" I squeak, "A _____ !" "Last question,"
               (verb ending in -ed)   (something in nature)

he declares. "Where does water leave its car?" I strain my parched brain. Nothing. Finally, I stand on my

_____ , and the answers trickles out. "A water park!" A(n) _____ blares and
  (body part)   (noise)

the _____ shakes. The fountain drops away, exposing a(n) _____ water park!
     (noun)   (adjective)

Sliding, splashing, and playing the rest of the day, I know I have never been so wet!

silly word beginning with "Y"

number

relative's name

adjective

kind of music

noun, plural

animal

direction

noun

noun

internal organ, plural

noun

verb

adverb ending in –ly

adjective

noun

noun

feeling

Crossing the Himalaya Mountains is taking forever. So are the endless jokes from _____

silly word beginning with "Y"

the yak. His jokes were fun, the first _____ miles. Too bad he is about as funny as _____ .

number _relative's name_

Plus, my funny bone froze hours ago. His impersonations include a(n) _____ pigeon, a tiger singing

adjective

_____ , sticking _____ on his head, and his wacky Aunt _____ . As we climb

kind of music _noun, plural_ _animal_

_____ the yak asks, "Hey, did you hear the one about...?" We yell "No more _____ !" so loud,

direction _noun_

we almost cause a(n) _____ . "What's with the jokes?" I ask. He says, "Laughter keeps you warm."

noun

By now, even my _____ are shivering, so I grab my _____ and

internal organ, plural _noun_

_____ _____ . Chuckles erupt from my _____ frozen friend.

verb _adverb ending in -ly_ _adjective_

Then his/her _____ sparks and catches on fire. I laugh so hard my _____ bursts into

noun _noun_

flames. Laughing the rest of the way, we are _____ and warm, though a bit charred!

feeling

SOME PENGUINS SLIDE ON THEIR BELLIES, USING THEIR FEET TO PUSH THEM FORWARD.

- adjective ending in –est
  - liquid
- verb
  - number
- verb ending in –ing
  - something cold
- body part
  - noun
- verb ending in –ing
  - number
- verb
  - noun
- friend's name
  - sound
- mythical creature
  - favorite song
- adjective
  - celebrity's name

Penguin Party

Walking along the Antarctic coast, I look for the _____ place to photograph.
adjective ending in -est

But I get too close to the _____ ! Ice starts to _____ , and before I know it—I'm adrift
liquid verb

on an iceberg! I turn to see black-and-white feathers. _____ pesky penguins gather on one end of the
number

iceberg and start _____ like it's a trampoline! Then, the _____ sloshes
verb ending in -ing something cold

over my _____ because our iceberg is tipping. *Splat!* A hefty penguin plops down and
body part

launches me so high into the air I think I see my _____ ! But I drop, _____
noun verb ending in -ing

on top of a(n) _____ -story-tall iceberg. I _____ down it faster than a(n) _____
number verb noun

and hear _____ _____ like a(n) _____ . Penguins jump
friend's name sound mythical creature

from iceberg to iceberg. I hear _____ and realize it's a flash mob—penguin style! The birds
favorite song

fling me back into the air, and I show off my _____ moves like _____ !
adjective celebrity's name

adjective

   noun

verb

   same verb

number

   type of container

something gross

   verb ending in −ing

animal, plural

   noun, plural

number

   noun

adjective

   friend's name

relative's name

   adjective

number

   same type of container

Fun Fact!

KANGAROOS
CAN'T HOP
BACKWARD.

Jumping Joeys

There are some _____ animals in Australia, found nowhere else on Earth. Walking to our
                    adjective

kangaroo observation tour, I remember I left my souvenir _____ at the gift shop. I _____
                                                          noun   *verb*

to catch the group, but I forget the guide's warning, "Never ever _____ near kangaroos!"
                                                                    same verb

_____ kangaroos spring into view. One puts me into her _____ , which smells like the
  number   *type of container*

inside of an old _____ . She takes off _____ over snapping _____ ,
                  something gross   *verb ending in -ing*   *animal, plural*

bounding through _____ , and vaulting _____ feet across a(n) _____
                  noun, plural   *number*   *noun*

—with me still inside! I peek out and see two other _____ -eyed "joeys" with their kangaroo
                                                     adjective

moms. It's _____ and _____ . Finally, the mama kangaroos stop in front of
            friend's name   *relative's name*

the _____ tour guide. They toss us to the ground and hop away. What a ride! I think I'll
      adjective

use the _____ cents I found in my kangaroo's _____ to buy everyone a snack.
          number   *same type of container*

adverb ending in –ly

  plant

number

  adverb ending in –ly

verb

  verb

noun

  famous explorer

country

  relative's name

silly word

  noun

friend's name

  animal

verb

  electronic equipment

verb ending in –ing

  verb

Fun Fact! **KOALAS** STAY AWAKE FOR ONLY **FOUR HOURS** A DAY.

Snoozing Through the Outback

Hurrying to the airport, we race through the Australian Outback. But we are so _____ lost.
(adverb ending in -ly)

I think we've passed the same _____ _____ times. Finally, in a panic, we stop to ask the
(plant) *(number)*

only living thing around, a napping koala. Jostling him awake, I beg for directions. It _____
(adverb ending in -ly)

_____ me a compass and a map. But the compass needle _____ like a(n) _____
(verb) *(verb)* *(noun)*

and the map was printed before _____ discovered _____ . The koala snores
(famous explorer) *(country)*

louder than _____ . I shake it, yelling, "_____ !" until the bleary-eyed beast
(relative's name) *(silly word)*

hands me a chart. Unfortunately, it was a(n) _____ chart. Frustrated, _____ whacks it
(noun) *(friend's name)*

with a stuffed _____ . Finally, the exasperated koala _____ into his pocket and
(animal) *(verb)*

pulls out a brand-new _____ , and instantly falls asleep again. _____
(electronic equipment) *(verb ending in -ing)*

we make the flight—just barely. I am so tired from our adventure, I _____ just like the koala!
(verb)

pet's name

   relative

something gross

   first name starting with "L"

electronic device

   verb

your street name

   adjective

verb ending in –ing

   color

yard tool

   friend's last name

feeling

   something slimy

animal

   noun, plural

body part

   verb

Fun Fact! WHEN FOOD IS SCARCE, GREATER DWARF LEMURS BECOME INACTIVE TO SAVE ENERGY, LIVING OFF FAT STORED IN THEIR TAILS.

Home, Sweet Home

What a trip! I miss being on the road, but am glad to have my _____ ! Even _____ 's
_____pet's name_____ _____relative_____

home cooking tasted better than the _____ stew we tried. I brought home a little
_____something gross_____

surprise, _____ the lemur. Before I can introduce my new friend to anyone, the lemur
_____first name starting with "L"_____

whips out a(n) _____ , then _____ it out the window. Bounding down
_____electronic device_____ _____verb_____

_____ , it snaps a shot of my _____ neighbor _____ . She turns
_____your street name_____ _____adjective_____ _____verb ending in -ing_____

bright _____ and throws a(n) _____ at us. Mrs. _____ isn't _____
_____color_____ _____yard tool_____ _____friend's last name_____ _____feeling_____

when the lemur accidentally knocks a bucket of _____ on her while trying to get an action
_____something slimy_____

photo. That makes the neighborhood _____ laugh so hard _____ shoot out
_____animal_____ _____noun, plural_____

its _____ . My lemur friend _____ a photo of that, too.
_____body part_____ _____verb_____

I haven't even unpacked yet, and my next adventure has already started!

47

Credits

Cover, Frans Lanting/National Geographic Stock; 4, karamysh/Shutterstock; 6, Michel Zoghzoghi/National Geographic Stock; 8, Eller/Shutterstock; 10, Iakov Kalinin/Shutterstock; 12, Daveallenphoto/Dreamstime; 14, Ntnstwin/Dreamstime; 16, Lanaufoto/Dreamstime; 18, VLADJ55/Shutterstock; 20, Lifeontheside/ Dreamstime; 22, Duncan Noakes/Dreamstime (Background), Duncan Noakes/Dreamstime (LE); 24, Zuzana Randlova/Dreamstime; 26, Doron Rosendorff/Dreamstime; 28, Herrbullermann/Dreamstime; 30, Nolte Lourens/Dreamstime; 32, Paul Topp/Dreamstime; 34, Vilainecrevette/Dreamstime; 36, Waj/Shutterstock; 38, Bbbar/Dreamstime; 40, Maxily/Dreamstime; 42, idiz/Shutterstock; 44, Joe Hubbard/Dreamstime; 46, art&design/Shutterstock.

Published by the National Geographic Society

John M. Fahey, *Chairman of the Board and Chief Executive Officer*
Declan Moore, *Executive Vice President; President, Publishing and Travel*
Melina Gerosa Bellows, *Executive Vice President; Chief Creative Officer, Books, Kids, and Family*

Prepared by the Book Division
Hector Sierra, *Senior Vice President and General Manager*
Nancy Laties Feresten, *Senior Vice President, Kids Publishing and Media*
Jay Sumner, *Director of Photography, Children's Publishing*
Jennifer Emmett, *Vice President, Editorial Director, Children's Books*
Eva Absher-Schantz, *Design Director, Kids Publishing and Media*
R. Gary Colbert, *Production Director*
Jennifer A. Thornton, *Director of Managing Editorial*

Staff for This Book
Kate Olesin, *Project Editor*
James Hiscott, Jr., *Art Director*

Kelley Miller, *Senior Photo Editor*
Ruth Ann Thompson, *Designer*
Ariane Szu-Tu, *Editorial Assistant*
Callie Broaddus, *Design Production Assistant*
Hillary Moloney, *Illustrations Assistant*
Ruth Musgrave, *Writer*
Jason Tharp, *Illustrator*
Grace Hill and Michael O'Connor, *Associate Managing Editors*
Joan Gossett, *Production Editor*
Lewis R. Bassford, *Production Manager*
Susan Borke, *Legal and Business Affairs*
Kayla Klaben, *Intern*
Angela Modany, *Intern*

Manufacturing and Quality Management
Phillip L. Schlosser, *Senior Vice President*
Chris Brown, *Vice President, NG Book Manufacturing*
George Bounelis, *Vice President, Production Services*
Nicole Elliott, *Manager*
Rachel Faulise, *Manager*
Robert L. Barr, *Manager*

The National Geographic Society is one of the world's largest nonprofit scientific and educational organizations. Founded in 1888 to "increase and diffuse geographic knowledge," the Society's mission is to inspire people to care about the planet. It reaches more than 400 million people worldwide each month through its official journal, *National Geographic*, and other magazines; National Geographic Channel; television documentaries; music; radio; films; books; DVDs; maps; exhibitions; live events; school publishing programs; interactive media; and merchandise. National Geographic has funded more than 10,000 scientific research, conservation and exploration projects and supports an education program promoting geographic literacy.

For more information, please call 1-800-NGS LINE (647-5463) or write to the following address:

National Geographic Society, 1145 17th Street N.W., Washington, D.C. 20036-4688 U.S.A.

Visit us online at www.nationalgeographic.com/books

For librarians and teachers: www.ngchildrensbooks.org

More for kids from National Geographic: kids.nationalgeographic.com

For information about special discounts for bulk purchases, please contact National Geographic Books Special Sales: ngspecsales@ngs.org

For rights or permissions inquiries, please contact National Geographic Books Subsidiary Rights: ngbookrights@ngs.org

ISBN: 978-1-4263-1355-4